The Stars and The Stripes

The Stars and The Stripes

The American Flag as Art and as History from the Birth of the Republic to the Present

BOLESLAW and MARIE-LOUISE D'OTRANGE MASTAI

Alfred A. Knopf   New York 1973

Except as specified in the List of Sources and Credits, all flags and related items in this book are from the collection of Mr. and Mrs. Boleslaw Mastai, New York, with special photography by Boleslaw Mastai and additional photography by Robert Brandau Associates.

Designed and produced by Chanticleer Press, Inc., New York, N.Y.

The text of this book was set by means of modern photocomposition. The text type selected is BASKERVILLE, the film counterpart of the original linotype BASKERVILLE designed by JOHN BASKERVILLE. The display type is AMERICANA, a contemporary handset derivative face in many ways similar to BASKERVILLE type. The Spencerian titling was hand drawn by GUN LARSON especially for this edition. This book was composed by TypoGraphics Communications and Haber Typographers, New York, N.Y., and printed and bound by Amilcare Pizzi, S.p.A.

THIS IS A BORZOI BOOK
PUBLISHED BY ALFRED A. KNOPF, INC.

Contents

Publisher's Note 8

Introduction 9

Acknowledgments 10

A Short Glossary of Flag Terms 11

The American Stripes 15

The First Stars 31

A New Constellation 43

Flag of the Seas 57

The Eagle and the Flag 83

The Starry Flower 99

Stars in the Storm 123

The First Centennial 157

The Flag in Daily Life 175

The Triumphant Banner 215

Constellation to Galaxy 231

A List of Official American Flags and Their Stars 243

A List of Sources and Credits 244

Index 245

Publisher's Note

This unprecedented book about the American flag reproduces for the first time the treasures of the unparalleled Mastai Collection.

For more than thirty years Boleslaw Mastai and his wife, Marie-Louise d'Otrange Mastai, have crisscrossed the country seeking out antique American flags — the rarest, the most beautiful, the most significant — as well as artifacts related to the flag.

Their vision of our national flag as a distinctive historical expression of American folk art stems both from their longtime professional involvement with the worlds of art and antiques and their passionate interest in Americana. Mrs. Mastai — born in Louisiana and descended from a colonial settler on whose seventeenth-century land grant a portion of Washington, D.C., now stands — is a painter as well as a writer, in both English and French, for leading art magazines. She served for many years as American editor of **Apollo** *and* **The Connoisseur** *and has also been curator of the Parrish Art Museum in Southampton, New York. Mr. Mastai, born in Cracow, Poland, is a lifelong antiquarian. He is publisher and editor of* **Mastai's National Directory of the U.S. Art & Antique Trade,** *which he founded in 1942. In addition, as an authority on the art of Poland, he has arranged exhibitions and published catalogues for major museums.*

For both the Mastais, through the last three decades, their search for the flag has been paramount. And it is their unending labor of love — finding, collecting, photographing, studying, and annotating "lost" examples of the Stars and Stripes — that has made this book possible.

Introduction

This book has come about because of our wish to share with fellow-Americans the result of a quest that began more than thirty years ago as a purely personal experience, although it concerned, it is true, a subject of common interest to all: the flag of our country.

It was then—with severely limited means and "leisure time" a euphemism—that we undertook to search out and acquire "old flags," as they were then called. This became in time the collection of antique Stars and Stripes and related items of which the major part is illustrated in this volume.

At first, our experience was purely pragmatic. We simply lived with and learned from the flags themselves. Soon we discovered, and became enthusiastic about, a phenomenon which we believe to be without parallel in any other age or country: in contrast to the ancient banners of Europe, ruled by strict heraldic laws since the twelfth century and made by skilled artisans, the irrepressible Stars and Stripes had been from the start left in the hands of the people of the United States. The flags had been not only homemade but home-designed as well. Americans had vied with each other in creating highly personal interpretations of their beloved flag—most of them unique, therefore—and in so doing they had been fully within the law. The strict regulations we now follow go back only one generation: during the earlier glorious epochs of American history, many variants of the Stars and Stripes were in simultaneous use. The flags generally set forth as atypical examples are, in fact, milestones in an exceedingly complex process of growth that extended over nearly two centuries. Yet, when we turned to the authoritative textbooks on the subject—the so-called "flag books"—we were disappointed to find that these were chiefly historical accounts, with no attention whatever paid to the artistic and social factors that intrigued us most. Nor did we recognize, in the rigid diagrams and reconstructions that served as illustrations, the hoary but very much "alive" old flags we had learned to love, every weathered fiber and faded tint of them.

We also found that museums and armories, insofar as they were concerned with flags at all, had been interested primarily in preserving flags connected with military history. There can be no doubt that this meant the loss and destruction of countless other precious examples. Regrettably, all flags are of their very nature ephemeral. Not only were antique Stars and Stripes exposed to many hazards in the course of their service but, when it was done, contemporaries would see little reason to preserve a worn-out and tattered flag. Such as have come down to us owe their preservation either to personal associations or to an awareness of their special beauty. In that double sense they may be looked upon, therefore, as both the rarest and the most exalted manifestations of American folk art.

Eventually, we came to realize that our own collection could furnish the bulk of suitable illustrative material needed for precisely the kind of "flag book" we had looked for in vain. Such a project, in addition, would call for a completely new approach, with the emphasis placed on the development of the *design* of the flag instead of on its history. To that end, we evolved a few broad classifications, grouping tentatively the major types of the popular flags and bringing some semblance of order into what had at first seemed chaos. For the same reason, we felt free to dispense with the usual chronological order whenever adherence to it seemed to confuse the over-all view of design development we were striving for. We have kept in mind that our main theme was the one aspect previously neglected by historians of the flag: the many-faceted personality of the Stars and Stripes at every stage of its exuberant, uninhibited growth.

Most certainly, it was an awareness of, and sympathy with, the unmatched freedom of the American flag that was at the root of our own interest in it—not only the freedom that the Stars and Stripes symbolizes now as ever, or even the freedom with which Americans used it in the past, but beyond these, in a very literal sense, the freedom of its design. For this is certainly the freest flag ever flown, with its scintillating stars and flowing stripes. That the two elements do spontaneously suggest movement is a thought that has been dormant for a long time, but was felicitously expressed as early as 1846 by John D. Long (later Secretary of the Navy) when he defined the essential quality of the Stars and Stripes as "the very poetry of motion."

Amagansett, New York
June 4, 1973

BOLESLAW MASTAI
MARIE-LOUISE D'OTRANGE MASTAI

ACKNOWLEDGMENTS

Our first thanks are due, by right, to Richard Feigen, not only because he was truly the first to grasp the meaning of this project but for his continued sympathy and interest in it as well. Very special appreciation goes to Anthony Schulte, of Alfred A. Knopf, Inc., who contributed what in our opinion is a well-nigh ideal title to a book whose purpose is, indeed, limited to the two elements of the American flag: the stars and the stripes. Our thanks go also to our editor, Regina Ryan, for her patient labor (great patience and much labor), and to our eagle-eyed copy editor, Donn Teal, for his valorous routing of ambiguities. We would also like to tender our personal gratitude to the various museums and other institutions which kindly granted the requests to allow reproduction of examples in their collections.

For additional assistance and helpfulness, our thanks go more particularly to: Richard Carter Barret, Director-Curator, The Bennington Museum, Bennington, Vermont; Florence Bundersen, Cataloguer, State House Library, Providence; Robert H. Burgess, Curator of Exhibits, The Mariners Museum, Newport News, Virginia; Herbert R. Collins, Assistant Curator, Division of Political History, Smithsonian Institution, Washington, D.C.; John M. Collins, Director, The Huntington Historical Society, Huntington, Long Island; Grace Cooper, Head, Textiles Department, Smithsonian Institution; Donald W. Corrigan, Librarian, U.S. Naval Academy Library, Annapolis; Leonard Denis, Executive Secretary, Pennsylvania Society of Sons of the Revolution, Philadelphia; Carl Dentcel, Director, Southwest Museum, Los Angeles; Richard Alan Dow, Rhode Island Development Council; Admiral George Dufek, U.S.N. (Ret.), Director, The Mariners Museum; P. W. Filby, Director and Librarian, The Maryland Historical Society, Baltimore; Eugenia C. Holland, Curator, The Maryland Historical Society; Edgar M. Howell, Curator, Division of Military History, Smithsonian Institution; John D. Kilbourne, formerly Curator, Historical Society of Pennsylvania, Philadelphia; Donald Kloster, Division of Military History, Smithsonian Institution; Albert T. Klyberg, Director, The Rhode Island Historical Society, Providence; Richard J. Koke, Curator, The New-York Historical Society, New York City; Richard M. Kuehne, Director, West Point Museum, U.S. Military Academy; John L. Lochhead, Librarian, The Mariners Museum; Jean Mailey, Associate Curator, Textiles Study Room, Metropolitan Museum of Art, New York City; Harold R. Manakee, Director Emeritus, The Maryland Historical Society; Mary-Paulding Martin, Director, The Star-Spangled Banner Flag House, Baltimore; Captain Dale Mayberry, U.S.N. (Ret.), Director, Museum of the Naval Academy, Annapolis; Mrs. Robert H. McCauley, Jr., Curator of Graphics, The Maryland Historical Society; E. Andrew Mowbray, Providence; Brigadier General William U. Ogletree, Fifth Regiment Armory, Baltimore; Wendy J. Shadwell, Curator, Mittendorf Collection, New York City; Ralph L. Thomas, Assistant to the State Record Commissioner, State House Library, Providence; Herbert P. Weissberger, Director of the Museum, The Society of the Cincinnati, Washington, D.C.; Conrad Wilson, formerly of the Manuscript Department, Historical Society of Pennsylvania.

A SHORT GLOSSARY OF FLAG TERMS

The authors have been asked to supply definitions, as a convenience to the reader, of some terms in general use throughout the book. They are happy to oblige but would like to make clear, however, that they most certainly do not wish to rush in where lexicographers fear to tread. Even Webster, for instance, very neatly eludes any exact definition of "colors," in the sense of "the national colors," with the vague description: "*pl.* a flag or banner of a country, regiment, etc." The Oxford Dictionary defines the term, similarly, as "a flag, ensign, or standard, of a regiment or ship"—which is all-inclusive but hardly specific.

Admittedly, the use of flag terms is very fluid. Even flag historians differ in their interpretations and personal use of such terms: one scholar has criticized as a redundancy the phrase "a naval ensign" used by another scholar. Yet the Oxford Dictionary still defines a standard as "a military or naval ensign." Who then shall decide when doctors disagree? (At any rate, it is of some value to be afforded this opportunity to point out that "union" is not a synonym for "canton"—nor is "canton" equivalent to "quarter.")

Canton—In the original heraldic sense, a term applied to the four square divisions placed one at each corner of a shield or escutcheon, and always less than a quarter of the total surface. The four cantons were identified as dexter (right) and senester (left), as well as chief (top) and point (bottom). At least five more divisions could be placed between the four cantons: chief, heart, point, and flanks (right and left). In modern usage, as applied to flags, the term "canton" has come to mean the division filling the upper inner corner of the flag—more specially in the Stars and Stripes, where it is rectangular instead of square, but also in other flags with the same composition, such as those of Australia, Chile, England, Greece, Liberia, and Uruguay. Colors—Initially, the actual colors used in the national flag, in badges, etc. This was meaningful at a time when color as a sign of recognition was all-important: one need only think of the Wars of the Roses in England. By extension, the term "colors" came to apply to the flags themselves, so that we now have "the national colors" and "the regimental colors"—that is, the national flag and the flags of the various corps. Ensign—The original meaning was a standard, or badge, of any kind, or even merely a symbol, or, literally, a "sign." In modern American usage, it is now restricted to the national flag at sea. Webster, however, still defines it as a "military or naval flag or banner." Field—The surface of a flag, but more particularly in its function as a background for the devices. The field of the canton in the Stars and Stripes is blue, and it bears white stars; the balance of the field consists of horizontal red and white stripes. Ground—The background color of the flag, or of any of its parts. Interchangeable with "field." Jack—A naval flag smaller than the ensign, flown at a ship's bow as a signal or as a mark of distinction, but more particularly in modern times to show nationality. The American jack consists of the canton of the national colors. This practice, however, is not invariably followed by nations who also have a flag featuring a canton in the upper right corner of the field. Greece, for instance, reverses it: the Greek national flag on land displays a large white cross on a blue ground; the Greek national flag at sea (which is also the merchant flag) has the same device in the upper right canton, and the rest of the field consists of nine blue and white stripes. Standard—Like ensign, "standard" originally had the general meaning of emblem or symbol. In heraldry, the term was more specially applied to a long, tapering flag—very much like a pennant—used as a "sign" by a king. In modern American usage, a military flag, more particularly cavalry colors. As indicated earlier, however, the Oxford Dictionary still defines it also as "a military or naval ensign." Union—The term was first used in reference to the union of England and Scotland in 1603, of their parliaments in 1707, and finally of the parliaments of Great Britain and Ireland on January 1, 1801. By extension, the term "union flag" was soon applied to the flag displaying the emblems of these nations, and the combination device itself became known as "the union." In turn, the American device of a group of stars, symbolic of the union of the colonies, was called the American union. The term applies solely to the device of union displayed in the canton, and is by no means a synonym for the word "canton"—although even eminent flag historians have sometimes used it in that connotation.

The Stars and The Stripes

The American Stripes

Contrary to still widely held belief, the flag of the United States did not spring full-blown into existence, the brainchild of an inspired seamstress in Philadelphia. Instead, as an early writer quaintly put it, "It was a creature of circumstances"—or, in the words of a modern historian, "a growth rather than a creation." The process of growth started considerably earlier than is generally thought but by no means harks back to the remote period when a flag was first raised on the North American continent—an event believed to have taken place in 1000 A.D., when Eric the Red or his son Leif raised the Viking sea rovers' banner (a black raven on a white field) on these shores. Neither this ancient Norse ensign nor any flag of the later European explorers and colonists, until the seventeenth century, took root in American soil; none of them was linked by the remotest design relationship to the future Stars and Stripes. The first inkling of things to come occurred with the arrival of English settlers in Jamestown and Plymouth. Their flag was the "red ensign," which held in a small white upper canton the ancient symbol of England:

Detail of the North Carolina Militia Flag (shown in full on page 39).

the Cross of St. George (page 17, number 1). In use since the time of Elizabeth I, the "red ensign" was likely the first national flag ever to carry the design combination of canton and field.

The basic compositional kinship to the American flag is already apparent, but it was soon to be brought one step closer. The stern Puritans of New England raised strong objections to the representation of the cross and did not hesitate to delete it from their own flags, leaving only the red field and a plain white canton (number 2). The result was oddly prophetic: the field ready to receive white strokes, the empty canton waiting to welcome a bright cluster of American stars. When the Cross of St. George was eventually reinstated on the "red ensign" about fifty years later, it was with a significant American addition in the canton: a small green tree symbolizing the forests of New England.

Probably at least one form of the "Green Tree Flag" was flown at the battle of Bunker Hill, but whether with a blue field or a red one has been the subject of much scholarly debate. Very likely it was a red field, since the colonists then still considered themselves loyal British subjects seeking nothing more than redress of their grievances and red was the color of England from time immemorial. Moreover, a Dutch flag chart of 1693 had shown the "Green Tree Flag" (identified there as "*le pavillon anglais de la Nouvelle Angleterre*") rendered with the heraldic notation (horizontal lines) for the color blue, but, as an afterthought or correction, this had been painted over with red; it was long overlooked that the Dutch text below the flag indicated the more frequent use of red for the field. In all likelihood, therefore, the "red ensign" with a green tree in the canton—the precursor of the Stars and Stripes—was indeed carried at Bunker Hill. The contemporary American artist John Trumbull, who was not only precise to a fault in documenting his paintings but also, to boot, a colonel of militia and therefore knowledgeable in such matters, has prominently depicted a "Green Tree Flag" with red field in his dramatic rendition of the battle at Breed's Hill.

Subsequently, the American patriots devised their own flags, and these were, according to a historian, "as various as the troops were motley." Commanders were expected to equip their corps with some form of identification, and both composition and expense were left to them. As a rule, their taste proved scholarly and aristocratic; they strove to emulate European banners but evidently did not realize that good heraldic art is severely stylized, for practical as well as artistic reasons, and eschews "storytelling." A typical example is the flag of the Thirteenth Regiment, of which only this description remains: "…ground light buff, device a pine tree and field of Indian corn emblematic of New England corn fields; two officers in the uniform of the regiment, one of them wounded in the breast the blood streaming from the wound; under the pine tree several children, one of the officers pointing to them with the motto 'For posterity we bleed.'"

In contrast to complex compositions of this sort, another famous standard, the Eutaw Flag, was distinguished by extreme simplicity. It consisted solely of a piece of crimson damask charged with romantic connotations, having been presented to Colonel William Washington by his fiancée, Miss Jane Elliott, who had improvised it from the upholstery of a dining-room chair. In time, this "maidenly guerdon," as a contemporary chronicler called it, became known as "Tarleton's Terror" from the high deeds of its troop in the field.

A group of early flags: (1) the "red ensign" of England; (2) the "red ensign" with empty canton; (3) the Moultrie Flag, 1776; (4) the flag of Washington's Life Guard, 1776; (5) a "rattlesnake" ensign, 1775; (6) the "Pine Tree Flag" of the floating gun batteries, 1775. None of these famed flags was a national flag; they served as provincial or regimental standards. Only the first two bear a basic design relationship to the Stars and Stripes to come, and paradoxically these were not, as one might expect, rallying signals for the patriots but were instead purely English flags in use long before the outbreak of the American Revolution.

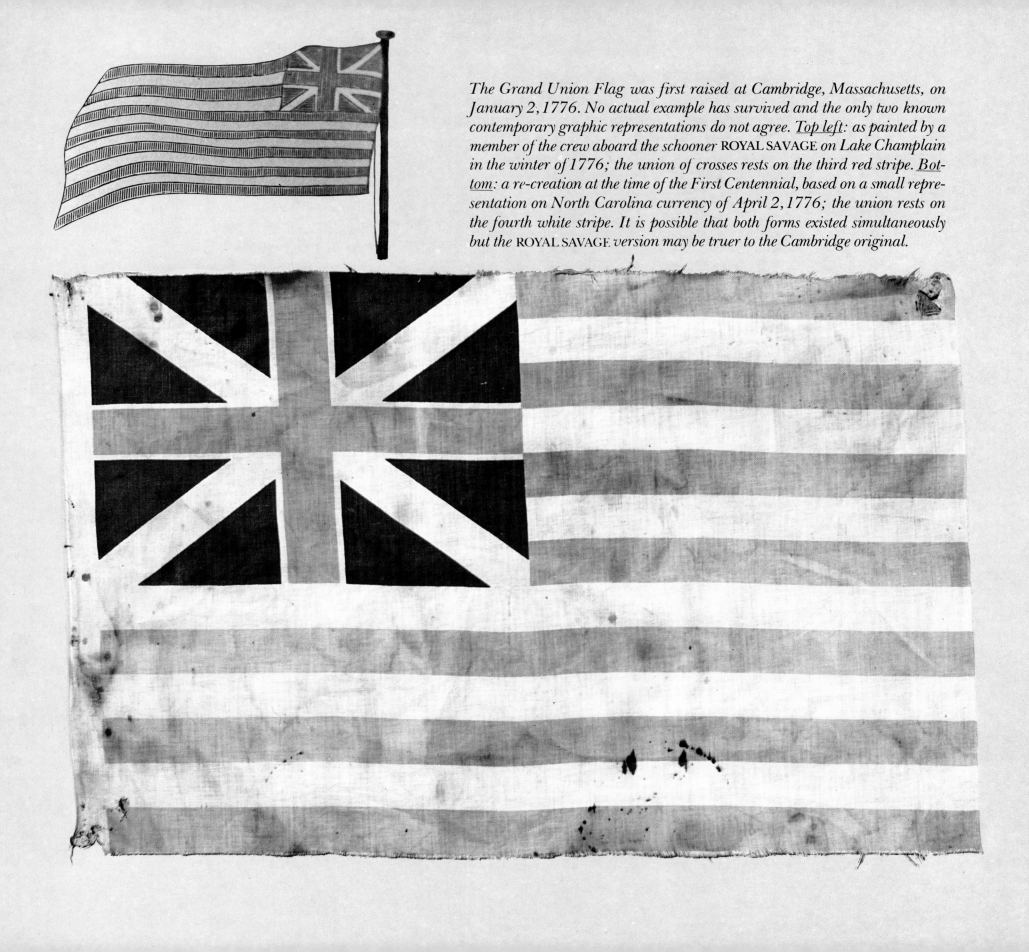

The Grand Union Flag was first raised at Cambridge, Massachusetts, on January 2, 1776. No actual example has survived and the only two known contemporary graphic representations do not agree. <u>Top left</u>: as painted by a member of the crew aboard the schooner ROYAL SAVAGE on Lake Champlain in the winter of 1776; the union of crosses rests on the third red stripe. <u>Bottom</u>: a re-creation at the time of the First Centennial, based on a small representation on North Carolina currency of April 2, 1776; the union rests on the fourth white stripe. It is possible that both forms existed simultaneously but the ROYAL SAVAGE version may be truer to the Cambridge original.

All such early flags were indeed flags of battle, closely identified with a particular leader and his follow-ers. But for at least one decade prior to the outbreak of the Revolution, flags of far more general signifi-cance had been flown as signals of ralliement for the patriots. Known as "liberty flags," and flown from liberty poles and trees, they had grounds of some plain color, or even white, and their essential feature was the word LIBERTY displayed on the field in large capital letters. At Taunton, Massachusetts, the word was flaunted boldly across the crimson of a British "red ensign" with its union of crosses. At Fort Sullivan (now Fort Moultrie), near Charleston, South Carolina, it gleamed on a blue field under the silver crescent that was the badge of troops commanded by Colonel William Moultrie (page 17, number 3).

One type of liberty flag associated more particularly with the "Sons of Liberty," a secret patriotic society, is known, however, to have had a ground striped red and white. This flag has often been re-created bearing the familiar horizontal thirteen stripes. In fact, however, some flag historians have described it as consisting of nine (in place of thirteen) vertical (in place of horizontal) red and white stripes. The only remaining use today of such vertical red and white stripes is in the oldest essentially unchanged American standard, the Revenue Cutters Flag of 1799, now known as the Coast Guard and Customs Flag (page 28); the Sons of Lib-erty played an important role in the Boston Tea Party episode, and it would seem natural and logical that their avant-garde flag of patriotism was transmuted into the emblem of the watchers at America's gates.

Vertical or horizontal, the red and white stripes of the flag of the Sons of Liberty may well have been the first instance of the use of stripes in a specifically American context—"the rebellious stripes," as the British branded them. The four white and five red stripes were symbolic of "45," the number of the pamphlet published in 1763 by the English civil-rights activist John Wilkes, whose influence on the American revolu-tionary movement was second only to Tom Paine's *Common Sense*. The numerical allusion, therefore, would have been as readily understandable to contemporaries as the upside-down "Y" in a circle—the modern peace sign—is to present-day Americans. Later, the symbolism of "9" came to apply to the nine states represented at the adoption of the Constitution on September 17, 1787—and also to the nine states which ratified it into existence.

Although the "American stripes" were destined to attain the dignity of national flag, they did not achieve this distinction at once. Their most serious rivals to that honor, however, were not those variations on the "thirteen" theme—thirteen arrows in a sheaf, the thirteen links of a circular chain, a sun with thir-teen beams, etc., none of which ever gained popularity. Instead, competition came from two conceptions widely different from any of these, and from each other. One was the "Pine Tree Flag," of simple dignity and beauty (page 17, number 6), with its solemn device AN APPEAL TO HEAVEN. The pine tree, however, had been too long associated with New England to be acceptable as a symbol common to all the colonies. The second contender was the rattlesnake, a purely Revolutionary symbol first featured in the *Pennsylvania Gazette* in 1754, when it served to urge union of the colonies. A truncated serpent, each writhing segment bearing the initials of one of the colonies, it was accompanied by the motto UNITE OR DIE. The emblem continued to appear thus, from time to time, until union had been achieved, but meanwhile on flags the dismembered reptile had welded itself into one sleek combative unit, menacingly coiled for attack as it hissed the defiant motto DON'T TREAD ON ME (number 5). While the truly mordant snake symbol admirably suited the early colonial mood of angry indignation, upon cooler consideration the "Rattlesnake Flag" would prove repugnant to many. The field would be left largely to the stripes.

The first documented Revolutionary appearance of the stripes is on the regimental flag of an elite Philadelphia troop composed of "gentlemen of property and reputation" and commanded by the Danish nobleman Abraham Markoe. This elegant standard of daffodil-yellow silk (page 21) bore in the canton, upper left next to the staff—heraldically the place of highest honor—a simple but highly effective device of thirteen horizontal stripes of blue and silver. As the Markoe troop accompanied General George Washington to Cambridge, Massachusetts, in mid-1775, and in November escorted Lady Washington there, it seems certain that the flag must have attracted special attention. On these occasions the resemblance that its device bore to the Washington coat of arms, with the latter's horizontal stripes of crimson and silver (page 21), must also not have gone unnoticed and may have played a role in the evolution of the national flag.

The precise stages of that evolution are unclear, but less than two months later the red and white horizontal stripes at last made their dramatic appearance. It was at Cambridge, Massachusetts, on January 2, 1776, where the militia troops of the united colonies had gathered to join into a true army under the command of General Washington. According to an Italian historian, Carlo Botta—whose *History of the War of Independence,* published in 1809, was based on eyewitness accounts—the American patriots, angered by a speech of George III, on this occasion publicly burned copies of it. They also decided to signify their rebellion by marking regimental flags (still the British "red ensign," with its canton of British crosses) with "thirteen lists symbolizing the number and union of the colonies." Although some historians believe that the striped flag had been determined beforehand by special congressional committee, Botta's account seems far more plausible. The colonies were, at that moment, still part of the British dominions, so what need was there to have preconsidered the creation of an official flag for a nation that did not yet exist? In Washington's own words, the improvised flag—which he termed the "Grand Union Flag" and which would be variously known as the "Great Union," "Cambridge," "Somerville," and "Continental" flag—was raised "in honor of the united colonies."

Under whatever name and for whatever purpose, it was an ambiguous flag of double allegiance: loyalty to the mother country, as symbolized by the British canton; devotion to the cause of the American colonists, as represented by the stripes. By an odd coincidence, the Grand Union Flag also chanced to be a duplicate of a British flag first flown by the East India Company in 1701—although, it is now believed, never in American waters. But if the East India flag was likely unfamiliar to American colonists, it was very familiar to British observers in Boston, who recognized it at once when it was raised in Cambridge and concluded, not unreasonably, that this "British" flag could only have been hoisted by the rebels in token of surrender. Thus

The Washington family coat-of-arms (<u>top left</u>) shows red and silver stripes (or, rather, bars) and five-pointed silver <u>molets</u> (spur-rowels), although the holes in the <u>molets'</u> centers are missing here as in most late American uses of the device—perhaps because of an unconscious national wish to identify them with the "American stars." The raven atop the crest is often mistaken for an eagle.

The silk standard of the Philadelphia Troop of Light Horse (<u>top right</u>)—presented to them by their captain, Abraham Markoe—is the first recorded instance of the thirteen "American stripes," although in the now-unfamiliar combination of blue and silver. As the troop escorted the Commander-in-Chief to Cambridge in 1755, it has been surmised that the simple but eloquent device of stripes as a symbol of American union may then have attracted Washington's attention and influenced the design of the national flag. The same device of thirteen blue and silver stripes occurs on two other regimental flags of the War of Independence—both of the 2nd Light Dragoons, Continental Line. The earlier—from the regiment's Connecticut period—has a blue field, while the second (<u>bottom right</u>) belongs to its New York phase (from 1777 to the end of the war). Once known as the "pink" standard because of its crimson ground, now totally faded, it is now called after the regiment's leader, Major Benjamin Tallmadge. These two dragoon flags may have been seen by Washington on several occasions.

Red and white was by no means the sole, or even predominant, color combination of early "American stripes." A privateer sported a black and yellow striped ensign (*replica, opposite page, top left*), while at Martinique in 1776 the brig REPRISAL flew a similar flag of yellow and white; the flag of the South Carolina navy joined stripes of Scotland's blue and England's red (*replica, this page, top right*). *Opposite page, bottom:* a tattered field of nine blue and white stripes is the treasured remnant of the "rattlesnake standard" carried by "Sullivan's Life Guard" at the battle of Rhode Island. *Top center:* in a watercolor of the siege of Yorktown, 1781, by British eyewitness Lieutenant Colonel John Graves Simcoe, the American flag appears to have blue stars on a somewhat lighter blue canton, and thirteen alternate red and blue stripes.

THE APOTHEOSIS OF BENJAMIN FRANKLIN AND GEORGE WASHINGTON (*bottom left*), 1785. Intended primarily as a tribute to the Philadelphia sage, this English textile nevertheless pays equal tribute to Washington, before whose triumphal cart—leopard drawn—an Indian herald waves the "American stripes." Guiding Franklin to immortality, the helmeted Minerva-like figure of America holds a great convex buckler adorned with fiercely pulsating multi-rayed heraldic stars. (The ultimate use, in the national flag, of severely geometric five-pointed *molets* cost us much poetic beauty in exchange for a gain in matter-of-fact delineation.) The image of Washington is after the mezzotint by Valentine Green, from John Trumbull's portrait; that of Franklin was inspired by the terra-cotta medallions of Jean-Baptiste Nini.

In 1801, the beautiful banner of the Society of the Cincinnati, at left (founded in 1783 by military companions of General Washington), continued the tradition of the blue and white regimental stripes that had been the first manifestation of this American device. A flag of the usual shape had originally been intended, but the two members who were appointed the task of designing it, Major James Fairlie and Lieutenant John Stagg, Jr., exercised laudable imagination and suggested, instead, the unique shield-shaped banner. It was made in New York City according to most exact specifications by a superlative needlewoman, a "Madam Bancel." Top right: regimental flags such as that of the Rhode Island Scituate Guards, from c. 1821, at times included variously colored stripes (probably carried over from an earlier, striped standard).

did the Grand Union Flag make its not too grand debut.

It may be that at least one other model for a flag of American union was brought forth on this occasion. According to Admiral George Henry Preble (1816–1885), foremost historian of the American flag, one Connecticut chronicler noted that at the Cambridge meeting "the red ground of the American flag was altered by thirteen blue and white stripes as an emblem of the thirteen colonies in war for liberty." The statement long puzzled historians, but assumed new significance with the unexpected discovery in 1921, in the port of Texel, Netherlands, of contemporary paintings of blue, red, and white striped American ensigns that were flown there by the fleet of John Paul Jones in 1779. This leaves no doubt, therefore, that a tricolor striped flag had been used at sea, and strengthens the possibility of a similar use by American land forces. In Trumbull's rendition of the surrender at Yorktown, the soldier-painter depicted precisely such a standard.

An interesting sidelight: in Europe the color blue was, from the late eighteenth century, associated particularly with the cause of American liberty. In 1789, the French Revolutionary orator Camille Desmoulins, addressing a Paris crowd, tendered them a choice for their rallying sign: "…green, the color of hope…or the blue of Cincinnatus, the color of Liberty, of America, and of democracy." In that year the tricolor flag of France made its appearance—precisely, in the now almost forgotten first form, with its bars in the sequence blue/red/white of the early American tricolor ensigns. Obviously, American use of tricolor stripes—or of stripes at all—came not from the influence of our French allies. On the contrary, the colors traveled from west to east, in good part a result of the Marquis de Lafayette's cherished American memories of "our dear, noble stars and stripes."

It would be a mistake to think that the "American stripes" were limited to the three colors red, white, and blue. In the early years of the Republic, the symbolism of the stripes proper, rather than their color, mattered most. The examples on pages 22–23 show something of the array of color combinations. Nor was the "color of hope" left out, as records exist of various green-striped American flags. The charge book of a Philadelphia ship's chandler lists, for December 20, 1775, "a Union Flagg, Green and Red, 13 stripes," while a bill found among the papers of the Governor of Delaware for 1783 includes "a piece of Green silk…for a Continental Flag"—this no less than six years after the red and white stripes had been officially established by the Flag Resolution of June 14, 1777. As late as July 4, 1807, in fact, the Volunteer Company of Rangers in Augusta, Georgia, was presented with a flag that bore "the accustomed device" but had "the stripes formed of alternate green and white."

Similar license would be taken in regard to the number of stripes. Nine, as well as thirteen, continued in symbolic use simultaneously with a number corresponding to the current number of states in the Union. Indeed, officially this role of the stripes in indicating the total states prevailed from early republican days. It is illustrated by an anecdote of the War of Independence reported in the London gazettes. An American privateer captured by the Royal Navy had been flying an ensign of only twelve stripes; the captain was asked the reason for the unusual number, and his interrogator quoted his reply, that, "since we [the British] had

In the decades before the Civil War, the "American stripes" became particularly associated with the reactionary current that gave rise to nativist movements such as the Know-Nothings, a secret society, later a political party, active from 1844 to 1860. The Know-Nothings, so-called because of their unvarying answer to all inquiries, professed a veritable cult for George Washington, to whose famous order "Put none but natives on watch tonight..." they assigned a bigoted sense. Their adulation is evident in a flag (<u>opposite page</u>) which displays on a field of seventeen stripes a portrait of Washington in place of the union of stars; the oval medallion was taken from a contemporary American textile (page 190). The Know-Nothing flag is signed and dated "J.W.L., Dec. 1858" (<u>detail above flag</u>). <u>Top left</u>: inspiration for a "new national song" was the murder in May 1844, by a rioting mob at Kensington, near Philadelphia, of young George Shifler as a result of his efforts to protect the American flag from desecration. The song, authored by an anonymous "Native," was so scantily printed that this is believed to be the only extant copy. The title sheet of the song bears a flag whose nine stripes evidence nativist conservatism, as does the smaller-than-ordinary canton. <u>Bottom right</u>: Shifler's death also inspired a rare lithograph. <u>Top right</u>: this "Washington banner" is another significant instance of nineteenth-century use of the first President's portrait, here on a field of "American stripes."

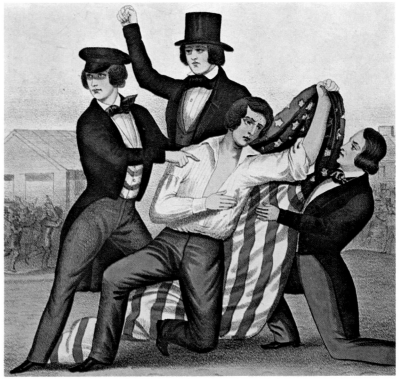

Sixteen vertical stripes (for the number of states then in the Union) were chosen for the field of the Revenue Cutters Flag in 1799 (*top left*) to distinguish it clearly from the national standard. The emblematic thirteen stars surrounding the eagle were blue, but there were no rules about their position: old illustrations show them in a circle, in an oval, in straight lines on two sides of the canton, in a fanlike double curve above the eagle, etc. Subsequently, this flag of sixteen vertical stripes became the Coast Guard and Customs Flag and the device in the canton was altered to an exact duplication of that in the Great Seal—the now-white stars grouped above the eagle's head in stellar formation.

The "American stripes" in a late revival (*bottom left*) provide a dramatic backdrop for the Stars and Stripes and its staunch defenders as well as for the flags of its allies. The national bird hovers majestically over all in this unusual "victory flag" celebrating the end of World War I.

taken New York, the Congress had a province the less; and that whenever they lost any of their provinces, it was their orders to cut away one of the stripes from their colors so that there should be no more stripes than provinces."

Lafayette spoke of "the stars and the stripes," and one wonders if he may not have been the first to describe the American flag in just that manner. In any event, by so doing, while he was following the rules of European heraldry—naming first the device in the place of honor—he may also have trespassed on an unwritten American rule. Officially the stripes were named ahead of the stars in every instance: in the original Flag Resolution of 1777, the second of 1795, and the Final Act to Establish the Flag, of 1818. Popular usage appears to have echoed gladly the phraseology of the lawmakers. The fathers who had conspired and fought under the "rebellious stripes," and their sons and grandsons after them, continued to give precedence to the older symbol—the stars, after all, were but an afterthought.

In some early flags, the canton of stars is so small as to suggest reluctance to include it at all (see the Fort Hill Flag, page 50). Benjamin Franklin and John Adams, as ambassadors in Paris, in answering European inquiries about the American flag, placed first emphasis on stripes, casually describing the canton as "a small square, in the upper angle next to the staff." Verbally as well as visually, the stripes would long maintain their supremacy. In 1814, Francis Scott Key, in a poem that would become the national anthem, hailed "*the broad stripes and bright stars*" of the Star-Spangled Banner of Fort McHenry. In 1829, an anonymous "national song" titled "Our Flag" (its author identified only as a messmate of Lieutenant James C. Calhoun aboard an American warship) exulted: "*Behold the glorious Stripes and Stars....*" In 1856, the composer Edward J. Allen urged his compatiots in similar terms to "*unfurl...the gleaming stripes and stars.*" In 1861—the opening year of the Civil War—Harrison Millard, in his exceedingly popular "Flag of the Free," hymned: "...*our stripes and stars, lov'd and honored by all,*" while another bard of that patriotic era, T. J. Donnelly, asserted ringingly: "...*never freemen yield,/ Under the Stripes and American Star,/ Under the Stripes and Liberty's Star.*"

The First Stars

Like the American stripes, the American stars have, as a separate heraldic device, no claim to uniqueness. Stellar motifs in some form or other have been in use since time immemorial, always as a symbol of man's highest aspirations. The star was first brought to Europe from the Orient by Crusaders, but its trail harks back even earlier to Byzantium—where it symbolized the Virgin Mary, "Star of the Sea"—and beyond that to Rome, Judea, Chaldea, Egypt: the stars of heraldry are almost as old as the stars of heaven. So fast did the Star, or *Estoile,* become an integral part of European blazonry that it soon attained a rank next only to the few ancient and essential emblems of that art's visual vocabulary— which, paradoxically, are known as its "ordinaries." From the start, the star of European heraldry was depicted with never less than six arms, or rays, these either wavy or sharply elongated ✳ to distinguish the star from a familiar emblem of Christian chivalry, the *molet* (rowel of a knight's spur), with its five broad triangular points ☆. Although as soon as the Stars and Stripes became truly the flag of the

Canton of the flag of the Green Mountain Boys (or Stark Flag, after General John Stark). The field, now lost, is said to have been sage green—New England's color.

American people, the *molet* was accepted as a star—and has remained one since—the six-pointed device has not only the prestige of heraldic tradition but as well the glamour of a long artistic history perhaps unparalleled by that of any other graphic symbol.

Artists have vied to bring forth personal interpretations of the star, variants ranging all the way from exquisite multi-rayed archaic stars, radiant and serene like small suns—which medieval and Renaissance painters placed over the brows of their Madonnas and cherubim—to the broadly pulsating, fitfully flashing meteors depicted by the designer of an eighteenth-century textile on the great concave shield upheld by the figure of American Liberty (page 23). This late, poetic interpretation came at precisely the time when scientific discoveries of the Age of Reason were sweeping away the picturesque imagery of the ages of faith and when the first telescopes were revealing the heavenly bodies divested of their mysterious halos of throbbing rays—"round as a button" they were, as the great astronomer William Herschel so uncompromisingly put it.

The traditional heraldic star was used occasionally in the American colonies. In 1680, a group of six-pointed stars was set around a central star of twelve rays on the seal of the town of Providence, Rhode Island; and even in 1676, stars of eight rays adorned the seal of Portsmouth in that same state (perhaps in remote relation to a stellar device on the arms of the town's English namesake). Rhode Island is, in this sense, the home ground of heraldic stars in America. But although efforts have been made to establish an unbroken continuity between the heraldic Rhode Island stars and the thirteen five-pointed "American stars" featured on several flags of the Rhode Island militia during the War of Independence, there is no doubt that Rhode Islanders understood the difference between the star and the *molet*. As late as 1781, when the name of King's County, Rhode Island, was changed to Washington County, the device chosen for its new badge was in fact not a star but a carefully identified *molet*—even to the extent of portraying an often neglected detail, the central hole through which the stem of a spur would pass. The reason for the choice of the *molet* was that it was part of the Washington family coat-of-arms (page 21). The choice, made four years after the passing of the Flag Resolution—which had prescribed stars as the device for the union of the flag—indicates that American patriots were then still clearly differentiating between the heraldic star and its five-pointed relative. The earliest Stars and Stripes (actual and pictured) invariably bear traditional heraldic stars, with six or more rays.

How then did the *molet* come eventually to replace the true star in American usage? There exists, of course, the well-loved but in the main mythical tale of Betsy Ross, the young needlewoman of Philadelphia. As that story goes, Betsy, having early in the Revolutionary period supposedly been assigned the task of constructing the very first Stars and Stripes from Washington's own design (actually the Betsy Ross legend, propagated by a grandson almost a hundred years later, never maintained that she designed the flag), made bold to offer a suggestion of her own—meant to facilitate not merely her current task but that of all future American flagmakers. With one snip of her scissors the resourceful seamstress demonstrated to her illustrious client that a five-pointed device was in fact much easier to make than the traditional form. Betsy's

Oral traditions to the contrary, the size of the great Bennington Flag very likely precluded its having been carried at the battle of Bennington, Vermont. It is more likely that it was hoisted over General Stark's encampment. A personal and unofficial interpretation of the Stars and Stripes, it is related, nevertheless, in concept and design to other historic regimental flags, in which emphasis was similarly placed on the canton and stars. The striking "arch" formation may have been charged with Masonic significance, as also the use of unique seven-pointed stars. Spun of sturdy Vermont flax, and presumably colored with home dyes, the flag has faded back almost to the natural tint of the fibers. Assuming, however, that the lighter and darker tones were once, respectively, white and red, then it appears that the stripes followed the heraldic order frequently used to the end of the Revolutionary period: alternate white and red, instead of the alternate red and white of modern custom. This great national relic was defaced in 1887 when a ruthless souvenir hunter cut off part of the top stripe and one star (on the side not shown).

A beautifully flowing, heraldically striped (alternate white and red) American flag appears on this Beauvais tapestry commissioned by Louis XVI of France in 1783 for presentation to George Washington. Before completion of the project, the French Revolution cost the king both his crown and head and canceled the gift. The French-American alliance is symbolized by a golden fleur-de-lys blooming above twelve five-pointed stars on a long, narrow canton of luminous sky-blue. Designer J.-J.-F. Lebarbier the elder consulted the Mondhare flag chart (Paris, 1781) for this "newest" of the world's pavilions (<u>at right, center and bottom</u>); the chart was mass-produced and crudely colored, but the devices were clearly discernible. <u>At right, top</u>: detail of another flag sheet, by Mattheus Seutter (Augsburg, undated), showing a fleur-de-lys atop a union of thirteen six-pointed stars that represent the "XIII Provinces" of America.

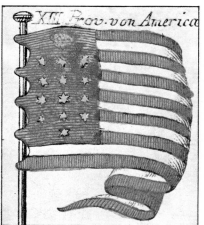

surprising familiarity with the *molet*—which was not well known in the colonies—may be explained by the fact that she is said to have done some embroidery for the Washington family. But if the difference between the two devices seemed unimportant to the simple Quakeress, unacquainted with heraldry, General Washington must certainly have known the difference and recognized the impropriety of using a device from his own blazon in the flag of the new nation.

It has, nevertheless, been suggested that the devices for the national flag were indeed originally patterned after the Washington coat-of-arms, which includes stripes as well as stars—or at least that the change from heraldic star to *molet* was made as soon as the resemblance was noted, in compliment to "the Father of His Country." But such adulation, although it appeared entirely plausible to succeeding generations, when the figure of Washington had become the object of a veritable cult, does not tally with what is known of the mood of the Revolutionary period. It is far more likely that the compliment would have been indignantly protested. Nor could any of Washington's close associates have been at any time ignorant of his emblazonry, for while he disclaimed any undue pride in his lineage, like any typical English gentleman of the period he displayed his crest on the panels of his coach, as well as on his bookplate, seal, and other personal articles.

Whatever brought about the transmutation of the stars into *molets*, it was at some time during Revolutionary times that the change took place. And while historians negate the possibility that Betsy Ross made the first Stars and Stripes, let alone designed it, they do know that she was employed in making flags for the Navy. Thus we may perhaps justifiably retain a small shred of the fanciful fabric of the Ross tale: that at some time in the course of her occupation Betsy may have initiated this easier way of mass-producing stars. It does sound so American, this converting of the proud heraldic device into a simpler, assembly-line pattern, and may thereby also be the first truly popular contribution to the making and designing of the flag.

A similar dearth of evidence exists in regard to the reasons, in the first place, for the choice of stars as emblems of the states joined together in solemn union. Stars may have been selected in the belief that the device had not previously been used by any of the states, and therefore could not be said to favor one state over another. But if this belief may have been influential, the choice cannot have been entirely fortuitous. The likelihood of Masonic influence—all-pervasive during the eighteenth century—certainly cannot be ruled out: the stellar design, pregnant with mystical significance, had long played a role in Masonic iconography, together with the arch, the compass, the pyramid, the All-Seeing Eye, etc. Washington himself was a high-ranking member of the craft, as were many others of the Founding Fathers as well as European supporters of the American cause. Masonic inspiration is suspected with good reason in at least two great historical starry flags: the Bennington Flag, with its arch (page 35), and the Pulaski Banner, with its esoteric symbol of the Eye within the triangle (page 34).

The first recorded mention of a star used in relation to the "American ensign" (the word "ensign" still carried the literal meaning of sign, or symbol, and was not yet limited to naval flags) occurs in some cryptic

The thirteen blue stars on this unusual homemade flag (<u>bottom left</u>) from New England appear to be of a solid tint only at a distance. A closer view reveals that the maker used various textiles each with a blue ground but with different small white patterns (<u>detail, bottom right</u>). The use of blue stars clearly points to militia use. The omission of the thirteenth stripe may not have resulted from a shortage of red material, but may rather have, like the privateer's flag described on page 25, indicated the temporary loss of a state to the British. Because of its fragile condition, the treasured old flag was brought out only on great occasions. One of these was the presidential campaign of 1880, when Winfield Scott Hancock (a former Civil War general) and William Hayden English ran on the Democratic ticket; at this time the band at the bottom of the flag was added.

HANCOCK & ENGLISH.

One myth associated with the birth of the flag is that the new standard immediately took its familiar place at the head of the American troops. Nothing is further from the truth. The privilege was granted to the various Army services only much later, beginning with the Artillery in 1834; the Cavalry, in 1887, was the last to receive it. A word of qualification: undoubtedly flags with the devices of stars and/or stripes have indeed been carried by American land forces since the War of Independence—but they were regimental banners, not national flags (even the familiar Cowpens Flag). It is reasonably certain that the flags depicted in battle scenes of the War of Independence by John Trumbull and Charles Willson Peale were also regimental banners. Frankly unorthodox arrangements of stars and stripes like those on this page were, therefore, not the result of eccentric whim, nor were they willful violations or erroneous interpretations of the Flag Resolution. These designs purposely make use of the American flag emblems, but with variations that distinguish them from the national flag. Top right: in the Easton Flag, the positions of the national devices are reversed. The thirteen small stripes in the canton recall the Markoe and Tallmadge standards (page 21), which probably did furnish the inspiration for this flag made in Easton, Pennsylvania, in 1814, for the "Northampton County Men" under Captain Abraham Horn. Bottom: the flag of the North Carolina Militia is reputed to have been flown at the battle of Guilford Courthouse, March 15, 1781. Thirteen great blue stars—eight-pointed— flash dazzlingly on its elongated canton, and the bold red and blue stripes of the field echo those of the early South Carolina ensign on page 23 as well as those of the flag pictured at Yorktown, pages 22–23.

This important Washington motif in tones of sepia on an ecru cotton ground, published "at Glasgow by C.G. in 1819," is based on an American drawing of 1783 entitled "A Symbolic Design Drawn by Charles Buxton, M.D." At the foot of the President's statue sit two large standards: an American flag and the French royal flag. The former displays fifteen stars on a white canton (fourteen are heraldic six-pointed stars, but the fifteenth is a five-pointed molet); the flag's field has twelve stripes, in the heraldic sequence white/red. On the other side of the statue, a ship wears an American ensign of stars and stripes but with only thirteen stars on a white canton in the unusual pattern of two rows of five stars each and one central row of three stars. In cartouches on the obelisks are (left) a figure of Columbia waving a minute Stars and Stripes and (right) Cupid brandishing another toward a discomfited Britannia whose own flag trails in the dust. Above Washington's head: the shields of nineteen American states out of the twenty that formed the Union in 1819 (Louisiana is, unaccountably, missing). It is presumed that the dark stars depicted throughout on various flags were intended to represent blue, although gold or even red cannot be ruled out. Significantly, all cantons are white.

lines published in the Massachusetts *Spy* on May 10, 1774, a little more than four years after the Boston Massacre: *"A ray of bright glory now beams from afar,/ The American ensign now sparkles a star,/ Which shall shortly flame wide through the skies."* Commemorating as it did the abhorred tragedy, the poem must have attracted more than usual attention throughout the colonies. It is conceivable, therefore, that it may have sowed the germ for the eventual adoption of stars for the flag some three years later. But this does not constitute proof that an actual flag adorned with a star was raised by the colonists as early as 1774. It is far likelier that the verses embodied no more than an ambitious metaphor. In a similar flight of hyperbole, the English "red ensign" was termed the "Meteor Flag" not because it included such a device but in allusion to the terror it struck in the foes of Britain. In the same mood, Americans would likewise later speak of their own rebel banner as "the meteor flag of '76." In 1774, however, any "American ensign" was as yet wishful thinking and could only sparkle figuratively with the brightness of hope in the eyes of rebellious colonists.

When the two devices of the stripes and the stars conjoined to form the national flag and the event was officially announced by the Flag Resolution, on June 14, 1777, the description furnished by the Congress was in the most general of terms. The union in particular was defined merely as "13 stars white in a blue field," without indication of shape, size, or arrangement. As far as we know, no actual model was prescribed — some historians see in this a proof that the flag was already familiar to all — and it was only natural that the "stars" mentioned would be taken to be the multi-rayed heraldic device that had always gone by that name. The color of the stars was indeed specified as white, though blue and gold stars were common in flags of the land and at sea the variety was even greater (see page 69).

Like the number of the stripes, the number of the stars faithfully reflected "the state of the nation." This was taken so literally, in fact, that an equivalent to the story of the flag of twelve stripes flown by an American privateer (see chapter "The American Stripes") details that, on April 20, 1789, when Washington passed through Philadelphia on his way to New York to assume the office of President, among the boats on the river all gaily bedecked in his honor, wearing their best colors, was one that flew a jack with but eleven stars, "representing the eleven states which had at that time ratified the Constitution."

It was the Star of American Liberty in whose semblance almost all modern stars would also in time become "American stars." Undeniably, the very few six-pointed exceptions remaining, such as those found in the flags of Australia and New Zealand, do somehow appear archaic and remote. It is whimsical indeed to reflect that even the Red Star of Russia and of China would probably have a very different look if, almost two centuries ago, the emblem of the young republic of the New World had not won from the nations of the Old the sympathy and admiration that eventually brought about the eclipse of the elder stellar symbol.

A New Constellation

On June 3, 1777, an unexpected petition was laid before the Congress assembled at Philadelphia. It was a request on behalf of the Indian Nation for "an American Flag." To expedite matters with it came "three strings of wampum" intended to cover the cost. The petitioners clearly were unaware that, almost a year after the Declaration of Independence, the former colonies did not yet possess a national flag. The Indian request may have spurred Congress to action, for eleven days later the now-famed Flag Resolution was enacted: *"Resolved That the Flag of the united states be 13 stripes alternate red and white, that the Union be 13 stars white in a blue field representing a new constellation."* The brief sentence—thirty words tucked in almost haphazardly in the overcrowded agenda of a harried wartime council—was deemed sufficient to announce a "happening" compared to which all other American historical episodes appear dwarfed. But if the statement was terse, it was not uttered casually or hurriedly. One crucial phrase was worded three times over. It is yet possible to see in the "rough journal" of Congress

Canton of thirteen stars in the pattern (shown in full on page 44) adopted during the Revolutionary period by the Third Maryland Regiment.

Only one contemporary record of a flag with all thirteen stars arranged in a "wreath"—the so-called Betsy Ross pattern—exists (in the background of a portrait of Washington by Charles Willson Peale). At the battle of Cowpens, South Carolina, January 17, 1781, a flag of related design was first flown by the Third Maryland Regiment; it bore in its canton a circle of twelve stars with the thirteenth star in the center. The flag at top left is of the "Third Maryland" pattern. Bottom: the superb vignette on a military commission signed by President Thomas Jefferson on February 23, 1808, shows (at right) a Stars and Stripes with fifteen stripes and fifteen six-pointed "flaming stars"—those of ancient heraldry, with arms of recurving flames. A jack (at left) repeats the canton of the Stars and Stripes at right. Behind the jack: a long flag with a canton of "American stripes," which are heraldically indicated as red and blue.

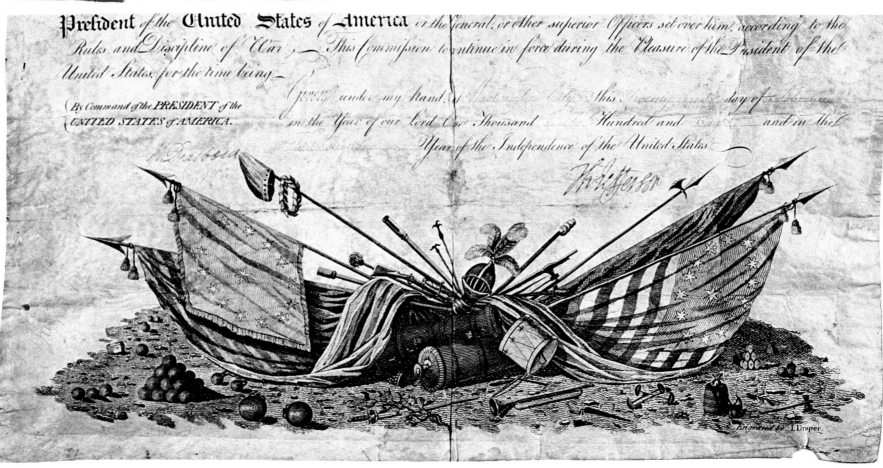

The "birth certificate" of the American flag—the Flag Resolution of June 14, 1777 (*top left*)—as it appears in the "rough" journal of Congress for that date.

In this detail of the map of Yorktown, 1781 (*top right*), by Major Sebastian Baumann, the Stars and Stripes is included among the array of regimental flags adorning the title vignette, but does not yet play the stellar role. (Compare with the Buell map, 1784, on page 48.)

The "square frame," or "square formation," pattern of stars seems to have been more popular than the starry circle. John Trumbull pictured it in final versions of two important works: THE SURRENDER AT SARATOGA, 1778 (*bottom right*) and THE SURRENDER AT YORKTOWN, 1781. Flags of the same pattern, worn by men-of-war and decorating Washington's barge in New York harbor, were portrayed by an anonymous painter of Inauguration Day, 1789.

In 1783, the celebrated Major Pierre L'Enfant, designer of the city of Washington, was asked to furnish a drawing suitable for illustration of the membership diploma of the patriotic Society of the Cincinnati. The result was a vast panorama in which the artist included a unique and elegant model of the Stars and Stripes, the thirteen stars of the "new constellation" placed in a graceful oval. This exquisite silk flag (<u>bottom</u>) follows the L'Enfant design precisely. The bright crimson stripes have paled to light coral, but the canton of midnight blue still effectively sets off the five-pointed "American stars," painted with gold dust in the manner of medieval illuminations.

the crossed-out variants: "that the Flag…consists of" and "…be represented by" evolved at last into the masterly fiat "that the Flag be…" The progression was from the commonplace to grandeur; one senses that the framers were fully aware they were addressing posterity.

It is generally believed that the project for a national flag had been under consideration for some time previous to the abrupt decision. A special committee had been appointed on the very day of the Declaration of Independence to prepare a design for the official seal of the new nation, and it is possible that plans for the creation of a national flag may have been initiated at the same moment. Certainly thoughts of the one item of national regalia may well have brought up thoughts of the other. Members of the Committee of the Great Seal included such personages as Dr. Benjamin Franklin, the Hon. John Adams, and the young but already famous Thomas Jefferson. In addition, the committee had secured the services of a learned heraldist, Thomas Barton, of Philadelphia, and of a noted French artist, Eugène Pierre du Simitière. It would be difficult to imagine a team better equipped to shoulder the double duty.

A puzzle, however, is that while copious reports were furnished over a period of six years on the subject of the development of the design for the seal, literally not one word appeared about a proposed design for the flag or about the reasons for the choice, in 1777, of the devices specified. Nor is there mention of credit due for suggestions or for art work prior to the adoption of the Flag Resolution. We do not even know why the resolution's original phrasing, "the Flag of the united states," was changed in a second version to "the Flag of the thirteen United States." The private papers of Charles Thomson, Secretary of Congress, might have shed light on these points, but regrettably he saw fit to destroy them all shortly before his death. These Revolutionary events were carried out with a great deal more secrecy than is now generally realized because of the Masonic affiliations of many participants, George Washington himself foremost.

Lacking more sober evidence, we can fall back on the opinion expressed in all seriousness by an old chronicler, that the two projects of the seal and the flag went on together because "it is a matter of natural history that 'the eagle lays two eggs in the first week of July.'" Of the two fledglings, then, one may say that the first was remarkably loquacious and its twin exceedingly reticent during the period of gestation. It is nevertheless patently impossible that the design of the flag could have been simultaneously conceived, perfected, and proclaimed on a single day by the Philadelphia assembly.

But, although the Flag Resolution established the identity of the flag, Congress would credit no particular author or authors. Completely discredited by historians is the tenacious legend that the Stars and Stripes leaped fully panoplied (about a year earlier) from the marble brow of the "Father of His Country," with Betsy Ross as midwife. One claim for the authorship of the design of the flag merits consideration, however. It was made contemporaneously and might, therefore, if spurious have been contested by witnesses at the time. It also derives additional weight from the brilliance and versatility of the claimant: Francis Hopkinson, an accomplished gentleman of the period, who was a gifted amateur poet and artist as well as a tried-and-true patriot and distinguished civil servant. His claim—and he presented it personally to Congress—was

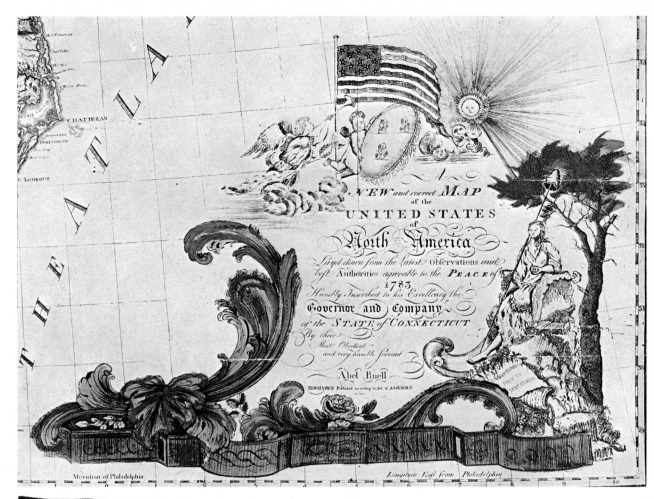

When Abel Buell offered his A NEW AND CORRECT MAP OF THE UNITED STATES OF NORTH AMERICA (_top right_) for subscription in New Haven, Connecticut, early in 1784, he described it as "the first ever compiled, engraved, and finished by one man, and an American." The proud Stars and Stripes, with like assurance, beams higher than the symbolical sun itself in his harmoniously balanced design.

Flying atop Fort Independence (then Castle William) in Boston, Massachusetts, this historic banner of thirteen stars and thirteen stripes (_bottom right_) received the first thirteen-gun salute tendered by a British man-of-war to the former rebellious colonies on May 2, 1791.

never denied; in fact, he came very near being awarded the modest compensation he asked for his "Labours of Fancy," as he called them. These included, in addition to the flag design, patterns for official seals and for Continental currency. Hopkinson requested "a quarter cask of the public wine," surely more as a token of recognition than as payment. Regrettably, he was never granted that satisfaction, Congress having finally resolved not to act, giving as reason that Hopkinson "had not been the only one to work on the project." It is now agreed that Hopkinson probably did originate the design of the first Stars and Stripes, in which the thirteen stars are in a "staggered" pattern technically known as quincuncial (see page 64) because it is based on the repetition of a motif of five units ⁙ . A "staggered" pattern would later be used sporadically, whenever the number of stars lent itself to it. Indeed, the pattern was revived, in our own days, for the flags of forty-nine and fifty stars.

Another reason for Congress's reluctance to acknowledge Hopkinson's claim may have been that, as evidenced by the Flag Resolution, no particular arrangement of the stars was specified: Congress was putting the problem squarely in the lap of flagmakers—the "new constellation" was a noble but nebulous figure of speech. Nor was a model furnished, as far as is known. Until the twentieth century, there was to be no precise official arrangement of the "American stars." Meanwhile, dissemination of the scanty requirements was surprisingly slow, the resolution not being reprinted by the press until three months later.

As late as 1795, when a "Second Flag"—of fifteen stars and fifteen stripes—was decreed, the design was still in metamorphosis. Its most illustrious example is the "Star-Spangled Banner," which inspired the national anthem (page 53). Theoretically, from 1795 on, both one star and one stripe were to continue to be added for each state joining the Union. But this was not always docilely observed. On the ensign of the frigate *United States*, a painting of which was done in 1798, there are still but fifteen stars and fifteen stripes (page 69). A widely practiced compromise began, which reflected the numerical increase of states only in the total stars. No doubt this was the easiest, cheapest, most practical way of bringing the flag up to date— whether by adding new stars to the old canton or, if not feasible, by replacing the canton.

That the Founding Fathers did not disdain economic considerations of this sort is demonstrated by the heated discussions that took place in Congress on January 4, 1795. Two new states, Kentucky and Vermont, had been clamoring for representation in the flag. Opinions were sharply divided, and the debate was characterized scornfully as "a consummate piece of frivolity" and "a trifling piece of business." Many members rose indignantly against the downright "sinful" waste of money the suggested change would entail—$60 for every vessel in the Union, one member specified. Others felt strongly, however, that it was important not to offend the new states—and perhaps even more so, for reasons of national prestige, that the world should learn in this guise of our continued growth. The latter won the day, in the teeth of a dire prediction: "If we alter the flag…we may go adding and altering at this rate for one hundred years to come. It is very likely, before fifteen years elapse, we shall consist of twenty states. The flag ought to be permanent."

Actually twenty-three years later, almost to the day, the Union did include twenty states, and again the

Heroic, rugged, highly individualistic, this homely banner flew over Fort Hill, Maine, during the War of 1812. The canton, with its fifteen casually spaced stars, has been reduced to the barest minimum—a narrow window on a wide sky. The overwhelming importance of the fifteen stripes is evident, as well as their devil-may-care irregularity.

question of a flag change was put on the table. This time, however, the subject was approached in a very different spirit. When the Hon. Peter Wendover, Democratic member for New York, rose on December 16, 1817, to suggest that a committee be appointed to draft the second change, it was already unanimously recognized that a further increase in stripes, with the resulting narrowing of their width, threatened to divest the flag of all dignity and meaning. To Captain Samuel C. Reid, a naval hero of the War of 1812, the designing of a new flag was entrusted. As a mariner, he was keenly conscious that thinner stripes meant proportionately reduced visual impact, and his first decision was to bring back the stripes to the original thirteen. Possibly with similar visual considerations in mind, he recommended that the stars should "be formed into one great star"—but that naval flags should have the stars in parallel rows.

In contrast to the reluctant acceptance of the flag of fifteen stars and fifteen stripes—destined, incidentally, to become one of the most glorious in American history—the flag of twenty stars and thirteen stripes was received with enthusiasm. Although it was not to have gone into effect until "the 4th of July next," the new "*bannered blaze*" (as a poet hailed it), the "banner of freedom" (as Congressman Wendover called it), was hoisted over the Capitol, in the new "Great Star" pattern, on April 13, 1818—an interesting instance of lawmakers being the first to disregard their own laws. But surely if any occasion warrented the transgression, this one did: the Act to Establish the Flag, of 1818, so well accomplished its purpose that any increase in the number of stars in the blue canton could henceforth only augment the beauty and richness of the American flag without disrupting its basic harmony.

Because it adheres so faithfully to the laws of European blazonry—not only are its fifteen stars six-pointed, but its fifteen stripes appear in white/red heraldic sequence—one wonders if the flag shown at top left may not have been made in England or France. It would seem that the flagmaker was told the number and color of the stars and the stripes, but saw no model. *Bottom left*: this unofficial banner of the transitional period between the thirteen-star thirteen-stripe and twenty-star thirteen-stripe flags retains the original thirteen stripes but shows sixteen jouncing and jostling rustic stars placed in an oval "wreath" with the seventeenth star at center. The flag was in the possession of the Hubbard family, of Connecticut, until recently.

The great Star-Spangled Banner, of fifteen "broad stripes" and fifteen "bright stars," was 30 feet wide by 42 feet long (*opposite page*). A good fifth of its field was torn away during its heroic vigil atop Fort McHenry. No explanation has ever been found for the odd checkmark-like sign sewn on the field.

The Act to Establish the Flag produced the prototype of the modern American flag, with its thirteen permanent stripes and as many stars as there are states. First flown on April 13, 1818, its twenty stars were grouped to form "a great luminary." Soon afterward, two consecutive presidential directives specified that the Navy should use, instead of the "Great Star" pattern: first (May 18, 1818), stars in parallel "staggered" rows; and second (September 18, 1818), stars in parallel aligned rows. The flag shown here (<u>front, this page; back, opposite page</u>) is believed to be the only twenty-star flag in existence.

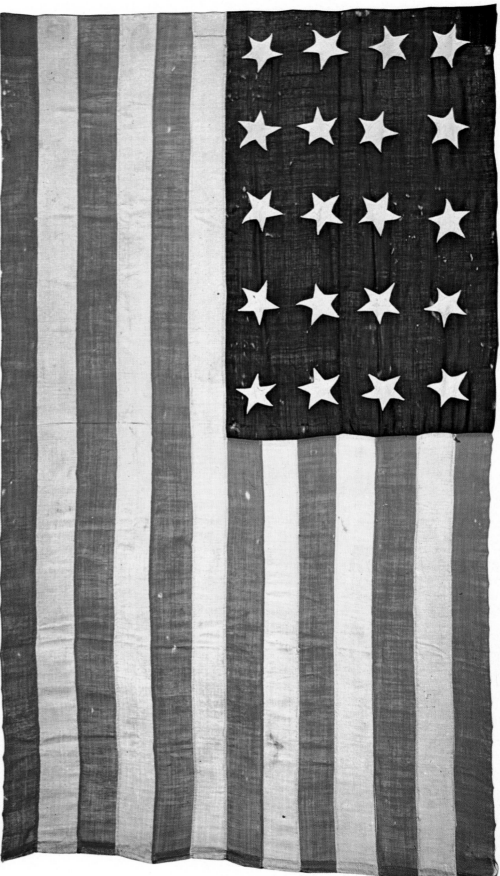

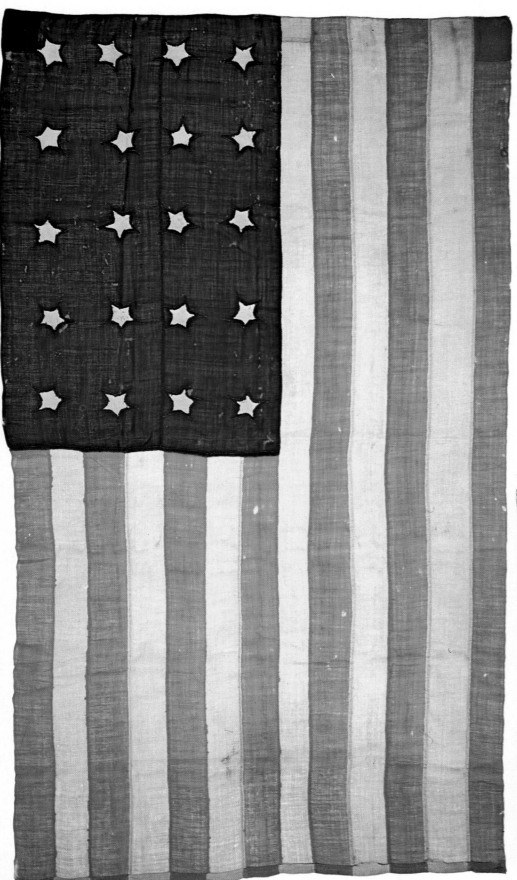

Antique flags of the pre-machine era—hand-spun, hand-dyed, handwoven, and hand-sewn, as well as individually designed—inevitably absorbed much of the human element during their creation. The two sides of the twenty-star flag shown here, in addition to subtleties of texture and coloring, possess distinct personalities: each handmade star was exactingly set on the front of the canton and the blue material was cut out on the reverse to allow the white star to show through—one star thus serving for both sides. The maker's hand likewise added liveliness to each star: not yet robotized by being set each at precisely the same angle, they still "dance" unrestrained.

Flag of the Seas

The nearest approximation to the word Yankee in Chinese is "Yong-kee"—two characters signifying "flag of the ocean." The coincidence is interesting not just because it was indeed over the ocean that our "starry banner" was brought by Yankee mariners to the great Empire of the East in the late eighteenth century, but because the Stars and Stripes was initially and primarily a flag of the seas. And for good reason. From the very start, the ocean had been the colonies' lifeline, an umbilical cord to the mother country. When the Revolutionary conflict erupted, George Washington categorically expressed his conviction that it was on the seas that American independence would be won. To that end, he personally initiated the formation of an embryonic war fleet. The need was urgent. Not only had the rebellious colonies decided to engage the world's greatest naval power, but while battling it they had also to protect an enormous, and enormously vulnerable, seaboard. America in fact *was* a seaboard, and little else—the thirteen "united states" must become a sea power or perish.

Canton of a thirty-one-star naval flag (shown in full on page 76).

The valiant little ships so hurriedly drafted could not compare to England's mighty "wooden walls" (as her war vessels were called) but they might well have been likened to the rude but effective stockades erected by the pioneers of the American wilderness: they did precisely equivalent service, holding at bay successively not one but two Goliaths of the seas—France as well as England—during the heroic period extending from the outbreak of the War of Independence to the conclusion of the War of 1812.

It was at the very outset of the Revolutionary struggle, in October 1775, that the first request for a signal of national identification was made on behalf of American ships of war by Colonel Joseph Reed, General Washington's military secretary. He wrote to the agents then outfitting the ships commissioned by Washington: "Please fix upon some particular colour for a flag and a signal by which our vessels may know one another. What do you think of a flag with a white ground and a tree in the middle with the motto: 'An Appeal to Heaven'? This is the flag of our floating batteries." Colonel Reed's suggestion was approved, but because of a shortage of "Green Tree Flags" (and indeed of almost everything else during those trying days) some American vessels had perforce to continue flying the Grand Union. Fairly soon, both flags were superseded by the "Rattlesnake" ensign and the "American stripes."

The short-lived "Green Tree Flag" did not necessarily show a pine tree—which was more particularly the symbol of Massachusetts—and at least one American shipmaster is known to have made a highly personal choice. When, on January 6, 1776, an American privateer was brought into Portsmouth, England, her captured colors, described with precision in the London *Chronicle*, consisted of "a pale green palm tree upon a white field, with this motto: 'We Appeal to Heaven.'" (The "pale" tint of the green was most probably a result of the sun-bleaching of the original color.)

The "Green Tree" ensign had done well enough for the floating gun batteries used on rivers and in closed harbors, but its qualifications for service on the open seas were doubtful. There, the few instants gained by swift recognition of friend or foe frequently spelled victory or defeat. And while green and white was a pleasant color combination, its visual impact was not strong; red was undoubtedly more effective, as the Dutch—those ancient and wise mariners—had long before discovered. In the mid-seventeenth century, they had elected to alter their national colors of blue, white, and orange to blue, white, and red, for the avowed purpose of optimum visibility at sea. Similarly, colonial seamen's practical considerations probably dictated the final choice of red and white stripes for the "American ensign."

From such sea wisdom, and because of the unusual simplicity of the pattern of the American flag—in an age still very much heir to traditions of heraldic intricacy—one is justified in concluding that the special requirements of the Navy were paramount for the flag's designers. Even the final exclusion of a motto tells of the Navy's influence: of questionable value on land, a motto was worthless at sea. But to support this naval influence we have something more than logic or conjecture, we have strong corroborative evidence.

First of all, the Flag Resolution is sandwiched in the records of Congress between various matters pertaining to the business of the all-important Marine Committee (including, notably, the appointment of Cap-

This pocketbook almanac (<u>top right</u>), shown in actual size, was published in Berlin in 1784. At the top of its left-hand page is one of only five known illustrations of American flags with tricolor stripes. Two others shown here are the Augsburg flag sheet (page 61), where the arrangement of the stripes corresponds exactly to this one, and the Serapis Flag (<u>watercolor, bottom right</u>), with its unique and erratic sequence of reds, whites, and blues. The almanac flag is an illustration in an article entitled "History of the Revolution of North America," by Matthias Sprengel, then Professor of History at the University of Halle, Germany. Based on eyewitness reports, the almanac article is the first account in German of the United States as a nation and includes its geography and descriptions of daily life and of each of the thirteen states. The article prophesies: "…our children and grandchildren will see and hear more of this new flag"; and categorically asserts that the representation of both the flag and the pennant is absolutely faithful, its accuracy having been verified by all thirteen states.

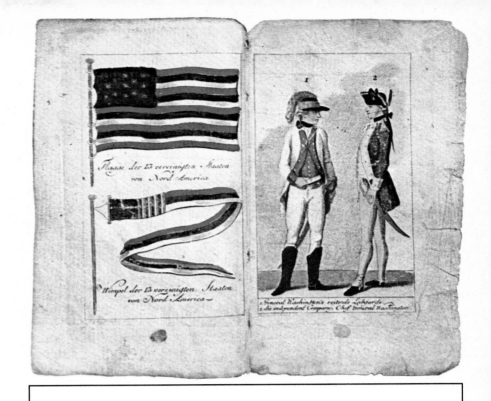

Watercolor representation of two "flags of the seas" (<u>bottom right</u>). The early naval Stars and Stripes shown above was flown in 1779 by the AL-LIANCE, a ship of the fleet commanded by John Paul Jones. The design is perfectly in accordance with the directions of the Flag Resolution and it complies also with every rule of heraldry: its top and bottom stripes are white (in contrast to modern usage) and its stars are not merely heraldic (here eight-pointed instead of the five-pointed <u>molets</u>, or spur-rowels, that would later replace them) but they are placed in a traditional "staggered" pattern known as quincuncial. John Paul Jones raised the flag shown below on the British frigate SERAPIS, which he had captured during the most famous Revolutionary naval combat, September 23, 1779, and to which he transferred from his flagship, the badly damaged BONHOMME RICHARD. When the victorious American fleet, including both ALLIANCE and SERAPIS, sailed into Texel, Netherlands, for repairs, the British minister demanded that the neutral Dutch authorities arrest Jones as a pirate. To refute that charge, the Dutch sought to establish that Jones was sailing under a recognized flag by sending an artist to make precise renderings of the American ships' flags. The Dutch script below the paintings indicates that the Serapis Flag was painted on October 5, 1779; the Alliance Flag was done the day before. Although the tremendous popularity which Jones enjoyed no doubt helped fix in the European mind the image of a tricolor striped American flag, contemporary European flag charts indicate that similar ensigns were flown by many American vessels of the period and suggest that the Serapis Flag was by no means as unorthodox as was once believed. The irregular color sequence of the stripes, however, remains a unique feature.

tain John Paul Jones to the command of the *Ranger*)—a clear indication that the subject of the flag must also have been within the jurisdiction of the committee. Here may be the answer to the mystery of the elusive "Flag Committee," of which no record exists: perhaps the two committees were one and the same, or perhaps the latter was a department, or division, of the Marine Committee.

There is, furthermore, the stubborn if unsubstantiated tradition according to which John Adams, "Father of the American Navy," is likewise reputed to have masterminded the flag project. In addition, Francis Hopkinson, when presenting his claim as designer of the flag, identified it as "the great Naval Flag of the United States" and "the Naval Flag of the States." Hopkinson, who eventually became one of the three commissioners of the Continental Navy Board, presumably knew whereof he spoke; in any event, his use of these terms was not contradicted. Further confirmation that the Stars and Stripes was primarily an ensign (in the modern sense; *i.e.*, a naval flag) comes by implication from Richard Peters, Secretary of the Board of War. As late as May 10, 1779, he worried: "It is not yet settled what is the Standard of the United States."

When, in 1817, it was seen that fundamental changes in the flag's design were unavoidable, Congress, as if in accordance with recognized tradition, again entrusted the task to a Navy man, Captain Reid, "the hero of Fayal." In the opinion of one historian, Reid "prized the stripes, an ancient naval signal, above the stars." No doubt he seized with alacrity the unexpected opportunity to reinstate the glorious and cherished "American stripes" to their original number of thirteen.

In time, the nautical need for clarity and boldness that had inspired the strong skeletal structure of the flag would be complemented and enriched by the spirited originality of seamen. And though the common sense and firm discipline of the maritime code continued to curb any overly eccentric fancy, to the play of forces—discipline and fancy—we owe some surprising interpretations (pages 77, 101, 113, 114) of the severely limited theme of two design elements (white stars and white stripes on grounds, respectively, of blue and red).

Recalling memories of his service during the War of Independence, the master of an American privateer was to reminisce how "at that time [1779] we had no national colors, and every ship had the right or took it to wear what kind of a fancy flag the captain pleased." Often too, in those times of dearth, it was the captain who supplied out of pocket the small arms and various other items of equipment, including the flag. To his wife fell the duty of making it.

While, as a result of the vague directions of the Flag Resolution, some startling but totally ingenuous misconstructions occurred, on the whole there seems to have been no willful intention to interpret independently the instructions issued by Congress, or to transgress them. The most famous instance—a true comedy of errors, now fully elucidated—was long believed an outright infringement of the congressional directive: the unique ensign with thirteen, tricolor stripes—blue, white, and red—in irregular sequence flown by John Paul Jones on the captured frigate *Serapis* (page 59). We know today that the unorthodox

Flag sheets were one of the mariner's most important aids in both war and peace. In this example, published in French in Augsburg, Germany, in 1793 — sixteen years after the Flag Resolution — the American flags (bottom row, center) are still shown with tricolor stripes in the same sequence as in the Sprengel Flag (page 59), and the stars are still the six-pointed heraldic. It is puzzling to find the tricolor stripes at such late date, not merely in the flag but in the merchant ensign and pennants as well. However, only one of the three pennants is multi-striped; the other two show, instead, three broad bars, in blue/red/white sequence. The most elongated of the three pennants carries, in addition, a device of vertical stripes that corresponds precisely to the arrangement depicted earlier in the pennant below the Sprengel flag. The fourth and last pennant in the row might easily be mistaken for yet one more American example but is in fact an erroneous rendering of the then brand-new tricolor ensign of the "Republic of the French." In an age that had seen two major revolutions, the blank spaces were allotted for additions or changes.

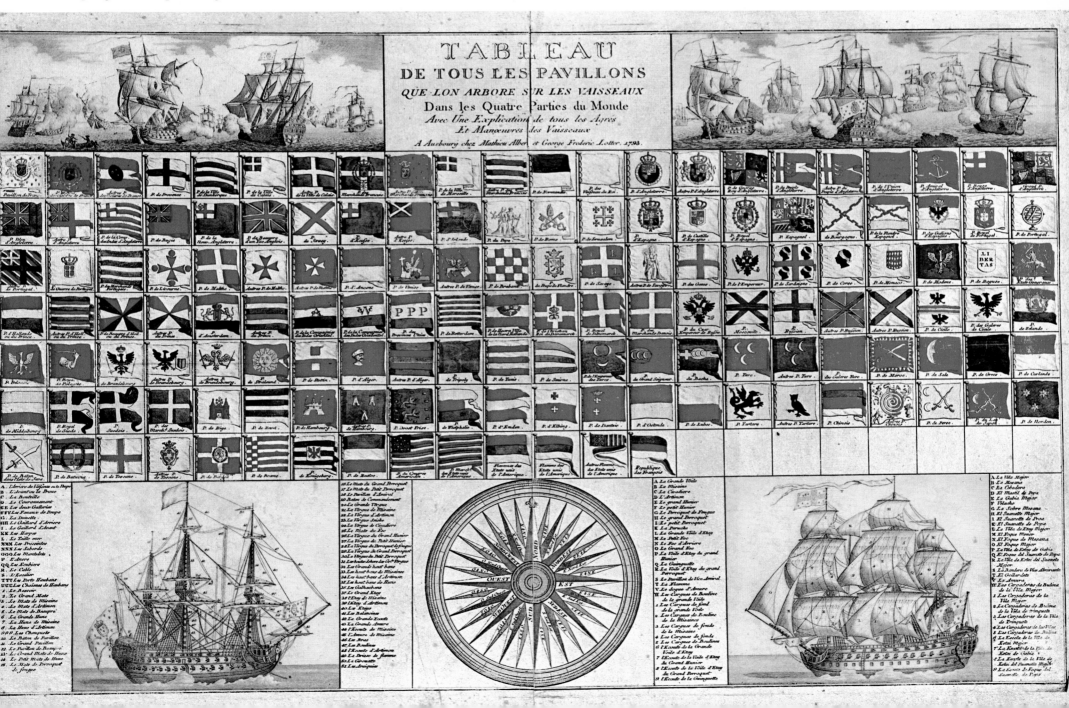

The "Prisoner's Flag" was found in Devon, England. It is believed to have been made by a seaman from an American ship captured in the Revolutionary period. Obviously improvised from material the prisoner had at hand, it is a small flag with stripes made of white silk ribbon, appliquéd to a ground of red wool twill of unusually fine weave—an officer's redcoat? The workmanship, and more particularly the embroidery of the stars, is typically masculine. The awkward patterning of the thirteen stars may have been intended to delineate the crosses of St. George and St. Andrew or a semicircular arch reminiscent of the Bennington Flag (page 35). The canton rests on the fourth red stripe, or "war stripe," as in the Serapis Flag (page 59). The probable original model for this wartime custom, followed during the War of 1812, the Mexican War, and the Civil War, is the Royal Savage Flag (page 18).

The significance of the nine stripes—in this sea captain's flag from the War of Independence—antedates the revolution, the number nine having played a role in the visual symbolism of the nation-to-be for possibly a decade before the union of the thirteen colonies. In 1763, English political reformer and colonial-rights champion John Wilkes, founder of THE NORTH BRITON, accused George III of falsehood and attacked John Stuart, Lord Bute, in issue number 45. As a cryptic reference to the inflammatory issue, "nine" (4 + 5) had deep roots in the popular consciousness by the time of the break with England. At times, as in this Revolutionary flag, the symbols nine and thirteen were combined.

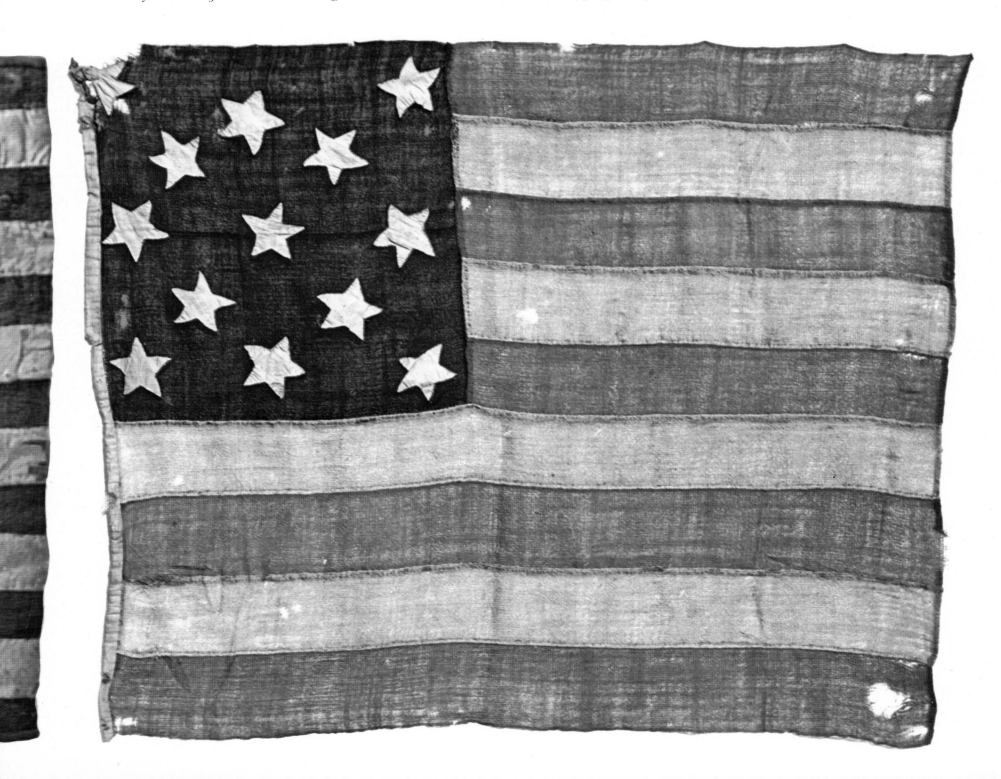

three colors of stripes were by no means a flamboyant eccentricity on the part of the naval hero, but were in strict accordance with the now little-known instructions released by Arthur Lee, one of our three commissioners in France. Lee wrote, on September 20, 1778, to Henry Laurens, then President of Congress, that a "ship's colors should be white, red, and blue alternately to thirteen, and in the upper angle next to the staff a blue field with thirteen stars." This is surprising, but even more so is the confirmation by his two colleagues in Paris, Franklin and Adams, who blandly gave similar information in answer to official inquiries from foreign ambassadors about the appearance of the American flag.

Almost one hundred years later, exact descriptions of Jones's two flags were found in the records of the island port of Texel, Netherlands, where the American fleet put up for repairs after the great naval combat in which the *Bonhomme Richard* "went down in victory." And in our own century, in 1921, paintings of the flags, done in Texel by order of the port authorities, were unearthed. These early naval Stars and Stripes still featured the traditional heraldic multi-rayed stars. But while these endured fitfully on land, they appear to have promptly fallen into disfavor for naval use, perhaps again because of overruling considerations of visibility: the multi-rayed stars blurred at a distance, whereas five-pointed *molets* proved splendidly unequivocal.

But the question why our commissioners in France felt it necessary to bestow, as it were, a special flag on the Navy has not been answered. Was it perhaps that the Stars and Stripes had already become established as the flag of the United States in the fullest sense? One thing is certain: American flags with tricolor stripes were flown not only by Jones but by other American vessels and merchantmen. The flag of the *Serapis* remains an inexplicable maverick primarily because of the irregular sequence of its stripes: blue/red/white/ red/white/blue/red/white/red/blue/white/blue/red. Was this because the flag was made hurriedly in replacement of the ensign that went down with the *Bonhomme Richard*? That great lost flag—great in every sense, for it was of large size as well as historically hallowed—was ecstatically described by John Kilby, a gunner's mate aboard ship, in an account unpublished until 1901: "The glory of America went up....I mean, the finest suit of colors I ever did see." His enthusiasm prevented him, unfortunately, from detailing whether it corresponded in design with either the *Alliance* or the later *Serapis* flags, or was yet another version.

Very few of the early naval Stars and Stripes have survived, doubtless victims of grievous wear and tear at sea or of wartime hazards. Fortunately, we can supplement their scanty testimony by turning to the paintings of specific ships made with near-photographic accuracy by highly specialized artists for the owners or skippers of the vessels. From a combined documentation—pictured flags supplementing actual survivors— an awareness clearly emerges of the robust personality of the youthful national flag at sea, its various facets, as it were, recognizable in the major types of patterning in the canton.

In early naval ensigns two patterns predominate, both exemplified in the Texel flags. The first is the "staggered"—in heraldic terms, *semé*—pattern, a quincuncial arrangement, which placed the stars in over-

Flag of the Seas

In this watercolor of the SOUTH CAROLINA, *signed "Jon. Phippen, A.D. 1793," the famous warship—first known as* L'IN-DIEN, *and prototype of the great frigate* CONSTITUTION—*flies the "American stripes" at topmast, as well as a most surprising version of the Stars and Stripes at the stern. The thirteen "stars" in the canton of the stern flag are actually crosses—oddly reverting to what is believed to be the most ancient of all stellar symbols. Paradoxically, this entitles the nonconforming ensign to the name sometimes applied to the Grand Union Flag (the predecessor of the Stars and Stripes): the "Crosses and Stripes."*

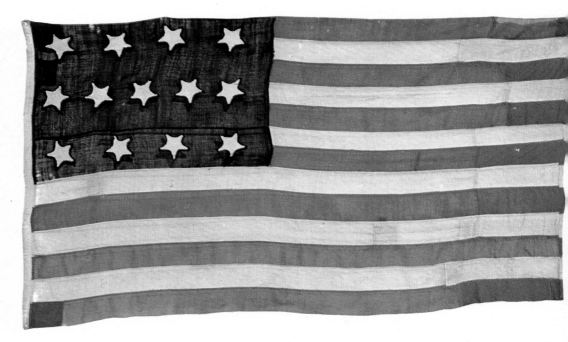

An early Stars and Stripes (reverse, or back, top right) flown on the famed Revolutionary privateer MINERVA eventually came into the possession of John Spear, skipper of the schooner NANTASKET, which was captured by the French in 1813. The flag is notable for its strong, well-balanced design. The three staunchly horizontal rows, or "ranks," of stars show an interesting detail: the bold truncating of the tips of the stars' rays on the obverse, or front, side of the flag (detail, opposite page), where they are inset in the bunting of the canton. The stars of the reverse side are therefore considerably smaller, because holes have been cut on that side.

In contrast to the Minerva Flag, another Revolutionary naval flag (bottom left) has its thirteen stars placed almost haphazardly. But these stars are appliquéd on both sides of the canton and are thus identical in size and shape (detail, top left).

lapping square or rectangular units of five (four corner stars and one central star). The use of a pattern based on the quincuncial arrangement inevitably results in a strongly diagonal effect (see the Alliance Flag), as is clearly evident in the present flag of fifty stars. In the flag of thirteen stars, this placement produced the unmistakable outline of the crosses of St. George and of St. Andrew, as used together on the British flag. Whether that result was willed from the start, or was merely accidental, it may have been the reason why, even at this early stage, the plainer fashion of placing the stars in three parallel rows (see the Serapis Flag) was preferred by many Americans to the quincuncial style: the arrangement avoided the suggestion of a still-maintained allegiance to Britain that had also told against the Grand Union Flag.

A third satisfactory solution was found in a pattern that may be described as "square frame" or "square formation," either with an empty center or with one larger central star (page 77). The first record of this pattern occurs in a painting by John Trumbull (page 45), while an early instance of naval use of the design appears on flags adorning the barge that ferried Washington across New York harbor in 1789, on the occasion of his first inauguration. Its pattern may hark back to the older Bennington Flag (page 35), whose corner stars suggest, if they do not actually outline, a "square formation." This rather severe arrangement endured from the neo-classical period well into the Victorian era—not surprisingly, for it is unusually well balanced, the solid center supplying (even with the occasional addition of a central star) a welcome area of visual calm in contrast to the effervescence of the rippling stripes. At times the rigidity of the "square formation" was softened by moving the corner stars slightly inward to achieve a curved effect (page 119). This transitional pattern stands midway between the "square formation" and the circular or oval "wreath" pattern.

Because the various patterns overlap in time, no exact chronological order can be established, although the flags do reflect with surprising fidelity the stylistic moods of various periods. At all times, however, flags of various patterns—and, not infrequently, of different numbers of stars—might be shown together without qualms. In 1815, the great ship *Constitution* was painted wearing both a large flag with the stars in parallel rows and a beautiful jack with its stars in a circular "wreath."

The "Great Star," or "Great Luminary," pattern, with all the stars grouped to form one large star, first attracted general attention when it was used for the first national flag of twenty stars, flown over the Capitol on April 13, 1818. In the Act of April 4, 1818, which had established this flag, there had been no provision made for the exact placement of the stars (history repeating itself!). Promptly on May 18, 1818, the Navy was advised by official circular that the stars should be arranged in a manner "you will perceive by subjoined sketch." The sketch indicated four parallel rows of five stars each, but with the second and fourth rows set back so as to bring their first star between the first and second stars of the row above—in other words, a variation on the old "staggered" pattern. Exactly three months later, the matter was reconsidered, and again by direction of President Monroe the Navy was advised that the stars should appear in parallel rows of five, but with the stars directly below those of the row above so as to form five vertical rows of four stars each. This was the pattern which Captain Reid had had in mind, from the start, for the Navy—the "Great Star" he

The frigate UNITED STATES *(gouache, c̲. 1798). Shown here in full dress, all contemporary national flags flying, the ship is portrayed as she appeared on the occasion of the celebration of her commission. The painting is one of several versions reputed to be the work of Patrick Hayes, nephew of her famed captain, John Barry.*

proposed was for the national flag as reserved for use on and in public buildings. In time the "Great Star" became the almost exclusive prerogative of the American merchant marine, which was not bound by these official Navy strictures.

A rare example, perhaps unique — certainly uniquely stark in conception — of the "cross" pattern (used earlier in the Hulbert Flag of the Revolutionary period) was depicted in 1850 by a maritime artist who showed the brig *Hamilton* (built in 1830) from Salem wearing a flag with its stars set in the form of a "Cross of St. George" — that is, the Latin cross, square-angled with even arms. The "cross" pattern was a basis for the "diamond," or rhombic, pattern, where a compact lozenge form was achieved by filling the arms of the cross with serried stars placed in parallel rows. The beautiful Irvine Flag (pages 112–113) — originally of twenty-nine stars, eventually increased to thirty-three — is a noteworthy example. The continued popularity of this design is exemplified by the famed flags of Fort Sumter, one of which is shown on page 125; both are of the basic "diamond" pattern, which appears at center with two starry columns at right and left.

In addition to the major patterns instanced above, there were other, more or less felicitous, individual creations. Admiral Preble summed up the ebullient creativity of those early days:

On the 4th of July 1857, a gentleman amused himself by noting the various designs displayed on vessels, hotels, and public buildings in New York. The majority of the ships had the stars arranged in five horizontal rows of six stars each, making thirty stars in all — thirty-one being the proper number at that date. Most of the foreign vessels, including the Cunard steamers, had them arranged, as heraldists would say, <u>semé</u>, that is, strewn over the union. Some had one large star formed of thirty-one small stars, and this style prevailed at places of public amusement and over the hotels of New York and Jersey City. Others had them in a lozenge, a diamond, or a circle. One vessel had one large star composed of smaller ones within a border of the latter; another carried the thirty-one stars in the form of an anchor; and yet another had this anchor embellished with a circle of small stars. Here were nine specimens of the flag alike in the thirteen stripes but varying in the design of the union. In addition to these forms I have seen the stars arranged in the letters U.S., and in other initials, those of the owner or company to which the vessel belonged.

But, Admiral Preble concluded somewhat wistfully, "It was just such dissimilarity that led the Dutch government twenty years earlier [*i.e.*, in 1837] to inquire without obtaining a clear and satisfactory answer: 'What is the American flag?'" (The patient Dutch certainly could not be accused of lack of perseverance. One recalls that they had been trying for an answer since 1779.)

In contrast to such early practices, the Navy in later years took to manufacturing its own ensigns, to ensure uniformity. Its end was achieved; but, unavoidably, the originality of our early flags of the seas fell victim to the dehumanizing effects of mass production. In the period immediately following the Civil War, maritime flags became standardized, and by the time of the proud celebration of the First Centennial, any spurt of creativity in flag design was evident chiefly on land.

A masterpiece of American folk art, this honey-colored tortoiseshell high comb shown approximately in halfsize (<u>top right</u>) was cut out and engraved by a whaler or sailor for his sweetheart back home. The military figure at left represents either Oliver Hazard Perry or Stephen Decatur receiving a laurel wreath from his grateful country; an eagle of victory alights on his arm. The fifteen-star fifteen-stripe flag stands between the naval hero and the allegorical Columbia, reclining on a martial drum. The stars in the canton of the flag are in the "square frame" pattern with one larger central star, a favorite arrangement during the Federalist era.

The thirteen-star "long pennant" (or pendant) at bottom is of the type worn well past the middle of the nineteenth century "at the main," according to Admiral Preble, "of all vessels commanded by officers below the rank of commodore and in the bows of their boats." This example differs from the type in that the stars are of even size instead of diminishing as the pennant narrows; also, the tip of the pennant is swallow-tailed instead of merely tapered.

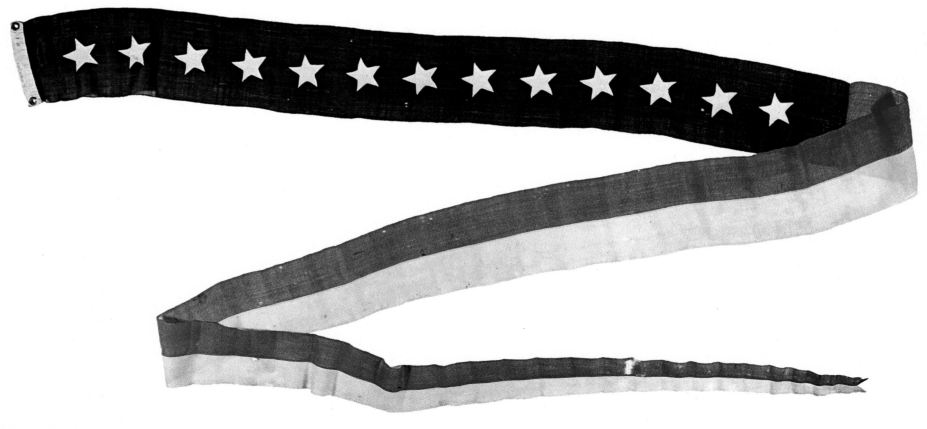

A ship's pennant emblazoned "Mary Eliza." bears a total of twenty-eight red stars on its top and bottom bands—Texas had come in as the twenty-eighth state on December 29, 1845. Ten additional stars of the same color arch in semicircle over an eagle, recalling the Revenue Cutters Flag of 1799 (page 28), and with three white stars on the eagle's shield represent the original thirteen states. An inscription on the side of the pennant reads: "James Udall, Great Neck"—the name of either the captain or the owner of the ship. Darning in pale blue wool and a red patch in the body of the eagle, as well as many other minor repairs, testify to the care that needle-wielding tars lavished on this beautiful flag.

The *"Great Star" flag opposite, of twenty-five stars (1836), was owned and flown by a Long Island sea captain.*

The romantic, adventurous era when great American clipper ships circled the globe, flying exuberant Stars and Stripes, is memorialized in a picturesque vignette (top right) that served as frontispiece for a twelve-section flag chart printed in Paris in 1836. An American flag is on the ship in the foreground, and an ensign with twenty-five stars in its canton is reproduced on one of the inner pages, together with an unusual version of the U.S. Customs flag in which the eagle is surrounded by a circle of stars.

The heraldic term _semé_ (literally, "seeded") describes a methodical sort of seeding, indeed, since it is meant to define the quincuncial pattern (see page 49). To describe the haphazard way in which the stars are set on the canton of this naval flag of thirty-one stars (_top right_) to form a dense, scintillating constellation evocative of a shower of shooting stars, one must coin a new term embodying precisely that conception: the "scatter" pattern. _Bottom:_ this cover, with its original hinges, came from an American seaman's chest. The sailor was very probably a crew member of the ship KATHLEEN, which he has proudly depicted on the chest cover surrounded by various national and signal flags — the Stars and Stripes in the place of honor. The KATHLEEN, built in Nova Scotia in 1854, was a four-masted bark with simulated gunports; that is, they were painted on the hold to deceive a possible predator as to the true strength of the vessel.

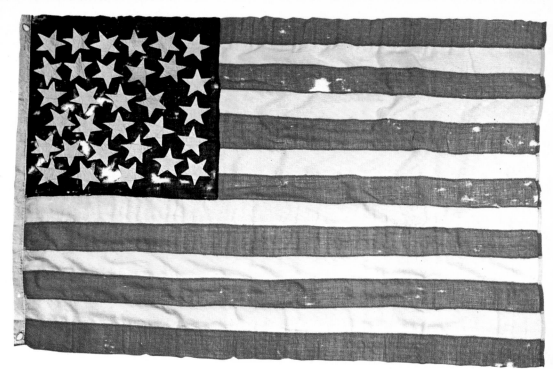

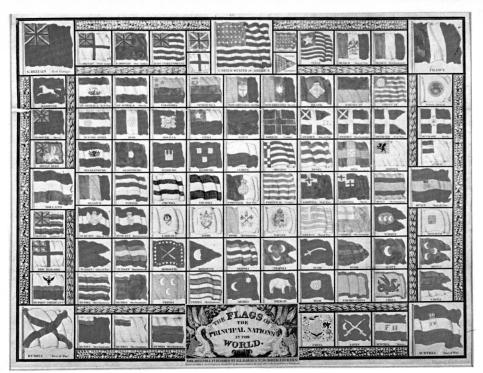

A chart (<u>top left</u>) of the "Flags of the Principal Nations of the World," published by R. L. Barnes, Philadelphia, 1837, is of the type used by American mariners at the time when "the white wings of our commerce" (in Admiral Preble's words) "began to expand all over the watery globe under the genial union of the stars, displaying them everywhere to the wondering gaze of distant nations and the furthermost isles of the seas." <u>Bottom</u>: the canton of this thirty-one-star flag displays a large central star framed in a double-square border of smaller stars, a variation of the traditional "square formation" pattern (already seen in the painting by John Trumbull, page 45, and in the tortoiseshell comb, page 71). Familiar on land in early days of the Republic, the "square frame" was more particularly a pattern of the sea. Flags with their stars in this striking pattern were flown by many American vessels as late as the mid-nineteenth century.

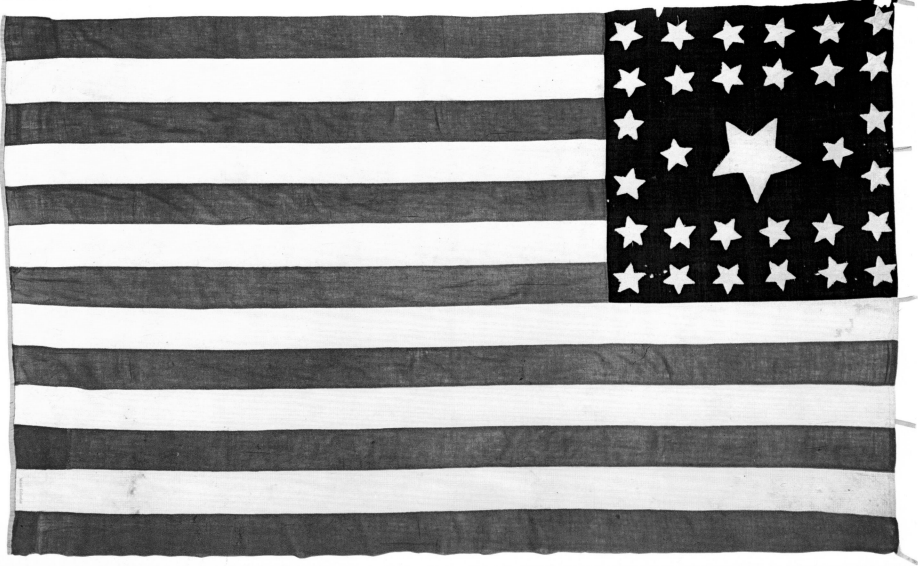

A monumental and sibylline Columbia in a painting of the 1870's (*top left*) serves as symbolic figurehead to the American ship of state, and significantly points to the swirling banner she upholds—where again one large star is set in the middle of a "square frame" of smaller ones. *Top center:* this graceful polychromed sculpture adorned the prow of the full-rigged iron ship BEN-MORE, built in Scotland in 1871. Conceived as a Cleopatra figure, she wears on her left wrist a bracelet-like golden asp. When the ship was transferred to American registry in 1921, the dusky Egyptian was transmuted into a fair Columbia and was garbed accordingly in the Stars and Stripes.

The MONITOR, after its victory over the Confederate armored vessel MERRIMACK, was glorified not only in song and verse but in art and crafts as well. Here (*bottom left*), a hooked rug made during the Civil War. The maker's somewhat telescoped view of the naval combat frankly focuses on the splendid flag atop the Union ship, where one large, effulgent star beams generously over a squadron of lesser stellar beauties. The flag's heavy, dangling tassels—certainly never used on the real MONITOR—contribute the final touch of Victorian opulence to the naïvely grandiose design.

The imminence of the Civil War cast an unexpected early shadow: a flag of eighteen stars, for example (<u>opposite page, top right; detail, this page, bottom</u>), was flown by the Hayes Arctic Expedition which left Boston on the schooner UNITED STATES *in 1860, when there were thirty-three states in the Union. It was long surmised that the flag had been made in the Arctic by a member of the expedition and that there had been a shortage of material. But the elegant design, professional workmanship, and unstinting proportions of the flag spoke against that supposition; furthermore, two pennants of the expedition each also displayed upper and lower bands (like the "Mary Eliza" pennant, page 73) carrying a total of eighteen stars. The solution to the puzzle lay in the custom, prevalent just before the conflict, to display on the flag the number of stars corresponding to the total states adhering to the respective causes. In 1856, Captain R. C. Davis of Charleston flew a flag of fifteen stars, predicting that this would someday be the correct number for the South. The flag of the Hayes expedition honored, by contrast, the eighteen states whose allegiance to the Union seemed unquestioned: the* UNITED STATES *would fly none but a flag of united states. (The central star of its flag presumably stands for Massachusetts, home state of the expedition.) Flown in the far north, the "Arctic Flag" shows bleached lines of strain, which stream like beams of polar light over the American "constellation."*

Exactly one hundred years after the Flag Resolution, this ensign (top) has its thirty-eight stars displayed in a "double-wreath" pattern that is not only graceful but meaningful: the inner ring consists of thirteen stars symbolizing the original states, while the outer ring groups stars representing the balance of the states that had joined the Union since its origin. One might judge the central star to be Guest of Honor—Colorado, admitted to statehood in 1876.

Like variations in a musical composition, the four jacks on the opposite page echo the basic motif of white stars on blue canton —but in varied manner. <u>Top left</u>: shown bannerwise, a jack of forty-four stars in the "staggered" pattern. This sparkling flag was flown on the famous yacht AMERICA. <u>Bottom left</u>: shown bannerwise, a jack of forty-five stars (1896), with alternate rows of seven and eight. Note the open ends of the jack: the stars of the three other jacks are nearly flush with their borders. <u>Top right</u>: shown as it would fly, this jack has two rows of nine stars both above and below a central row of eight—totaling forty-four (1891). <u>Bottom right</u>: shown bannerwise, the earliest of the four jacks (detail) pays only lip service to symmetry: its vertical rows are somewhat askew and its irrepressible stars tilt at different angles. All four jacks are of wool bunting, with hand-sewn appliquéd stars.

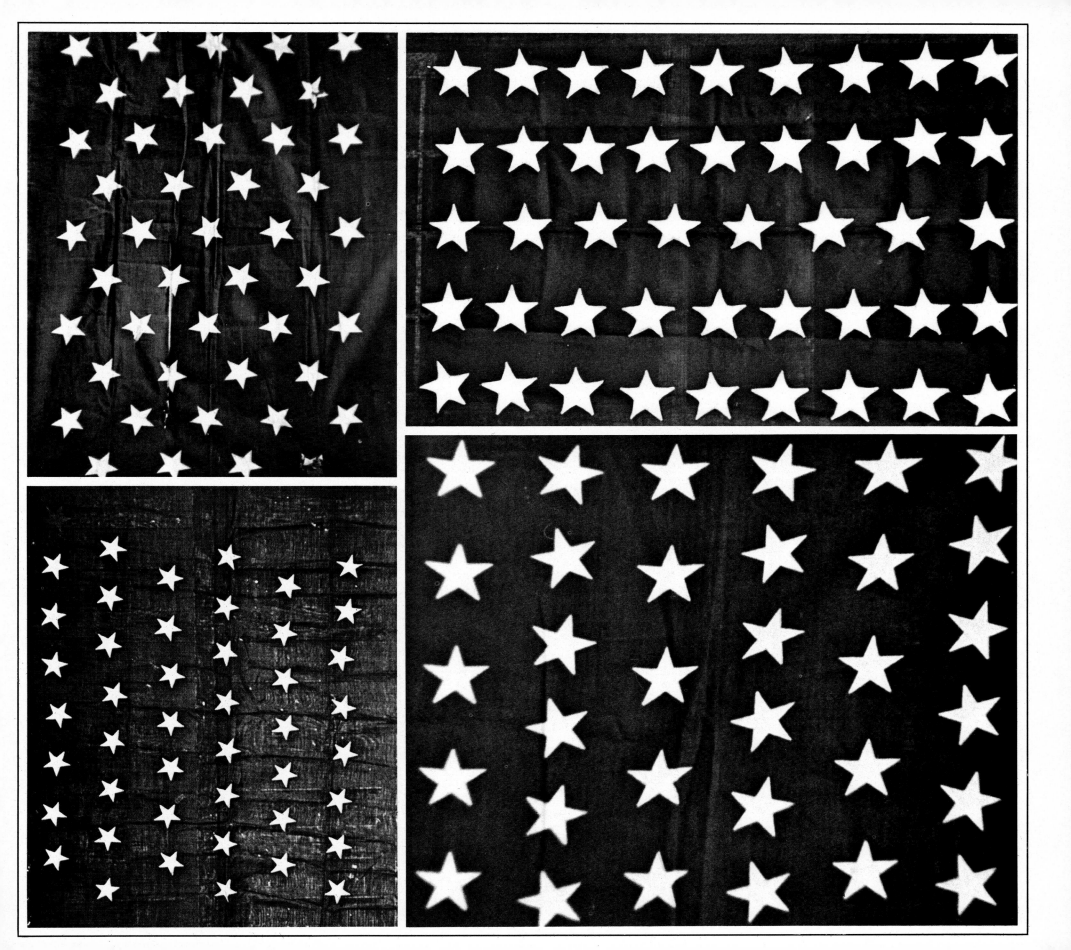

The Eagle and the Flag

In 1734, a delegation of Creek Indians, sent to England by the directors of the Georgia Company, was headed by an aged chief, "Tomo Chachi, Mico, or King, of Yamacraw." He is portrayed in a very fine mezzotint done in London at about that time by a Dutch artist, together with his young nephew, "Tooanahowi, son of the Mico of the Etchitas." The brave, some ten or twelve years old, clutches possessively and fearlessly against his bare breast a truly royal pet: a splendid white-headed American eagle. The Indian patriarch himself solemnly presented George II with some eagle feathers, commenting that they came from "the Swiftest of Birds...who flies all round our Nation....[They] are a Sign of Power in our Land...and we have brought them to leave with you as a sign of everlasting peace." While this is believed to have been the first documented instance of the eagle's role as an American symbol, according to an ancient tradition pre-Columbian tribes had already raised as a standard "a pole full-fledged with the wing-feathers of an eagle." Inevitably the colonists must in time have come to share the feelings

Canton of the famous Frémont eagle flag (described on page 96).

An EMBLEM of AMERICA.

Published 4 Sept 1798, by John Fairburn, 146 Minories, London.

This enchanting personification of the young nation of the New World is still endowed with all the graces of the Old: with her blue scarf, pink gown, and softly powdered hair— an attenuated version of red, white, and blue, "the colors of Liberty"— she is utterly of the eighteenth century in mood. Quite in keeping, too, is the delicate heraldic standard she holds on a long, slender staff. On a white field with rose-colored stripes, a golden eagle spreads its wings and talons in true heraldic fashion, and in the canton a dainty constellation sparkles like some precious jewel of diamanted filigree on a ground of azure-blue enamel. Entitled "An Emblem of America," this aquatint, finished by hand in watercolor, was published on September 4, 1798, by John Fairburn, 146 Minories, London.

of the aborigines for the great bird which at that time indeed still flew "all round our Nation." Interestingly, Benjamin Franklin raised strenuous objections against the adoption of the eagle as our national bird. Not content to brand it as "a bird of bad moral character" (not without some justification, as naturalists concur) but also as "a rank coward" (which is more questionable), he went so far as to suggest, in preference to the handsome raptor, the homely turkey, a harmless and beneficent native fowl. But it was a matter in which, for once, Dr. Franklin was not to have his way. The prestige of the eagle was too great and too ancient.

In the Old World, the eagle had long been revered as a symbol of supreme power: as the bird of Jove in ancient Greece, as the golden symbol of Rome and of Byzantium…Fierce double-headed eagles were used on the standards of the Hapsburgs and Romanovs; the sinister black eagle was revered by the Teutonic Knights; and it was representing the proud and spotless white eagle of Poland that Casimir Pulaski and Thaddeus Kościuszko had so readily come to the aid of the American patriots. Against all this glamour and splendor, Franklin's vehement objections proved of little weight, and the eagle was assigned the stellar role in the heraldic cast of the Great Seal, or Seal of the United States. Thus was established a visual symbolic link between what was in truth the "Empire of the New World"—for was it not composed of thirteen sovereign states?—and its peers of the Old World.

From the outset, the connection between the eagle and the flag was indissoluble. It is significant that one of the many preparatory designs submitted for the Great Seal showed the eagle holding in its right talons a thirteen-star flag, while the left brandished a naked sword. In this early conception of the eagle theme, the flag played the role now assigned to the olive branch.

Flags with a field of stripes but with an eagle in the canton in place of stars may have been used as early as 1781, and it has been supposed that the Great Seal was taken from such flags. But this does not tally with the well-documented history of the designing of the seal, an exceedingly laborious process begun in 1776 and concluded only in 1782. Moreover, the sole evidence for the use of the eagle design on flags prior to the seal is that such flags were shown on a French medal depicting the battle of Cowpens (1781)—a medal struck in 1790. The artist may well have been misinformed, or else may have used the standard purely symbolically. As late as 1801, an English artist showed a figure of "America" holding a standard combining devices of a rattlesnake on the blue canton and a golden eagle with spread wings on the field of multiple "rebellious stripes" (page 196).

The use of the rattlesnake and eagle together is not as surprising as it might seem. As late as 1799, there is formal mention of a flag "with the Union and Emblem in the center…and the regimental number and State in the curve of the serpent"—a clear indication that some form of "rattlesnake ensign" was still under consideration for, if not in actual use by, the Army. The eagle was destined to supplant the serpent, however, and the enthusiasm with which the final design of the Great Seal was welcomed probably played an important part in this. The flag we now call the Stars and Stripes was still considered primarily a Navy flag, and what could have been more natural than the evolution of a distinctive flag for the Army: the eagle flag—

"flags with an eagle in the canton," or "eagle canton flags," as historians rather ponderously call them.

The first recorded instance of the making of an eagle flag is found in the diary of Dr. Ezra Stiles, President of Yale College, who both described and illustrated it. In 1783, some patriotic ladies of New Haven, Connecticut, including the wife of Roger Sherman, had undertaken to make, at considerable expense and trouble, "a grand silk flag" to be displayed at a "Public Rejoicing for the Peace." In the upper canton of a red-and-white-striped flag, "the arms of the United States" were to be figured: *i.e.*, the Eagle with Shield. The ladies, however, took as a model for this a sumptuous heraldic design embossed on the cover of a Bible printed in Philadelphia, which they assumed could be nothing less than the national arms. It was, in fact, merely the arms of the State of Pennsylvania—an error immediately pointed out to them by Sherman upon his return from Congress. Meanwhile, the maverick flag was displayed and "appeared well."

The American Army had been disbanded promptly after the victorious conclusion of the War of Independence, Congress being anxious to avoid the slightest imputation of militarism. Before two years had passed, it was evident that the move had been premature, and that the new nation still needed the protection of a standing force. So great, however, was popular repugnance to the use of the very term "army" that the new contingents raised received, instead, the rather transparent synonym "the Legion." Under whatever name, the troops needed flags—not only company flags, but a common Army standard.

General Knox, head of the Legion, made an interesting suggestion for an unusual sort of "super-flag," which he proposed as a "Standard of the Legion." His description was of "a bald eagle formed of silver and large as life." This has been somewhat tamely interpreted as the usual flat device, embroidered or painted in silver color, but one wonders whether General Knox, in keeping with the neo-classical tastes of his age, may well have meant a representation in the round of an eagle—literally "formed of silver"—such as were carried at the head of Roman legions. Knox's eagle would have been more grandiose, in fact, since it was to have been life-size. Regrettably, nothing seems to have been done to carry out his suggestion.

In 1818, Captain Reid, paradoxically a Navy man, volunteered at the same time as a design for a national flag of twenty stars and thirteen stripes a lesser-known idea for a flag he termed precisely "a national standard." The standard was to be divided into four equal parts (an ancient heraldic practice). The first upper quarter retained the stars, but the quarter next to it featured the design of the Great Seal—that is, the eagle device. The lower tier was to have the Goddess of Liberty in the quarter immediately below the stars, while the quarter next to it was to contain the thirteen stripes. Like Knox's heroic eagle, Captain Reid's "national standard" remained in limbo.

Two years later, the eagle came into a unique—and non-flag—use. At the instigation of John Quincy Adams, then Secretary of State, the arms of the United States were displaced from the American passport by an unusual interpretation: "the Eagle with the Lyre." For the next 150 years, Americans would travel under the aegis of the national bird in this somewhat unexpected guise, bearing on its kingly breast a great

LIBERTY

This magnificent soaring eagle gripping in its talons "the banner of Liberty" was painted by an anonymous artist in the early years of the Republic. At a time when self-taught limners all too often came close to portraying, instead, Benjamin Franklin's alternate suggestion (see page 85) — if not some even scrawnier, more ludicrous bird — the eagle shown here is marked by genuine grandeur. The sun rising over a tall mountain range doubtless symbolizes the dawn of American independence.

The Standard of the Eagle

This oldest national color bearing a regimental number—the "standard of the eagle" of the U.S. 1st Infantry Regiment, 1791—is incomparably beautiful. Its extreme delicacy of coloring and execution is fully worthy of the poetic conception: the eagle rises serene and effortless, in true Olympian majesty, against an unusually harmonious pyramidal sunburst (or "glory") while eight-rayed stars, as intricate as flowers, scintillate softly in the depths of a night-blue sky.

GOD ARMETH THE PATRIOT.

Two great merchant ships flying eagle flags make their way toward docks of Yankee merchant prince John Cannon, in this VIEW OF THE CANNON HOUSE AND WHARF (*top*) by Jonathan Budington (active *c. 1792–1812*). Atop the medieval-looking fort also flies an oversized flag of seventeen stripes, of the period 1803–1812, though the flags' cantons, resting on the "war stripe," point to the later date. The eagle canton may have been adopted by the Cannon fleet because of the widespread popularity of the Great Seal device in the late eighteenth century.

In this silken banner (*bottom left*), presented by the Ladies of Nashville to the Nashville Battalion during the Creek Indian war of 1813, the delicacy of the floral border is in decided contrast with the austere scriptural motto. As in all early "standards of the eagle," the stars are still heraldically six-pointed. The spread eagle with short wings is also of the heraldic type, and in fact recalls the Brandenburg eagle of some of the flags surrendered at Yorktown. Indeed, one historian has written that "even our enemies bore gifts to us in the way of heraldic suggestions."

The splendid standard (<u>front, this page; back, opposite page</u>) of the Washington Guards, a corps of Massachusetts militia formed in 1810, was presented to the troop on July 4, 1838. Painted in oil colors on silk, the flag is of such high artistic caliber that it is obvious the donors commissioned an artist of repute. Very far indeed from the plainly garbed figures of more recent versions, the Indian on the Massachusetts shield is still

PRESENTED BY THE LADIES, JULY 4TH '38.

E PLURIBUS UNUM

WASHINGTON GUARDS

in every sense a "noble savage." The radiant symbolic star to which he points is heraldically six-pointed, as are the twenty-six white stars in the flags on each side. The twenty-six gold stars around the eagle are set as morning stars in a silvery pale-blue firmament—an interesting departure from the night-blue backgrounds usually found in "standards of the eagle" (see page 88).

The Kingsboro Flag, like the Frémont Flag (page 82), has twenty-six stars, though in every other respect they are in contrast. An unusual feature is the azure fan above the eagle, with the stars in three graduated tiers. The thirteen stripes appear in the heraldic sequence white/red. The flag is obviously the work of a trained artist justly proud of his work: he signed his name, HOLMES, in capital letters across the tips of the bird's tail feathers. As early as 1818, the Russian artist Paul Svinin portrayed a similar eagle flag in his TRAVELS IN NORTH AMERICA. Opposite page, top left: an eagle flag remarkably similar to the Kingsboro Flag is shown in this scene drawn on October 19, 1851, by Rudolf Friedrich Kurz at Fort Union, on the Missouri River. The eagle grasps a calumet, as on the Frémont Flag, but as in the Kingsboro the eagle occupies fully one-third of the entire field. The nine stripes are also in heraldic sequence, as in the Kingsboro Flag. Top right: in the martial eagle flag of the 4th Indiana Volunteers, from the Mexican War, the canton rests on the "war stripe" and the eagle proffers solely arrows of war. Bottom right: this Chinese eagle embroidery of the late nineteenth century is notable for its golden tonality.

"Old Abe," the famous "battle eagle" of a Civil War Wisconsin volunteer regiment, was immortalized in word and picture (see page 96). On the cover of a period music sheet (<u>bottom left</u>), the cherished mascot perches on the special stand on which he was carried at the head of the troop. <u>Bottom right</u>: California had joined the Union two years earlier, and the eagle on this 1853 music sheet is the tawny-hued golden eagle of the Southwest. A unique convex shield with converging stripes sheathes the body of this warrior eagle, while his talons hurl thunderbolts instead of arrows. <u>Opposite page, top left</u>: a mid-nineteenth-century American eagle tapestry with silver beading. <u>Bottom left</u>: a headquarters flag from the Civil War combines the features of a "standard of the eagle" (a national color) with those of an eagle flag (defined, page 85). Above the initials in the canton (for Department of the Cumberland, a military district), the stars are set in an unusual pattern of overlapping ogives. The golden eagle is a purely heraldic representation, closely related to the one on the 1813 regimental flag (page 89). <u>Top right</u>: in contrast to the uncompromising eagle on the 4th Indiana Flag, this eagle, on tapestry, proffers the olive branch of peace. The tapestry was made for sale at the "Sanitary Fair" of 1864, sponsored by President Abraham Lincoln for the benefit of military hospitals. <u>Bottom right</u>: in the final quarter of the nineteenth century, visits by our fleet to the Far East, as well as droves of American tourists, occasioned such Asiatic interpretations as this high-relief Chinese embroidery eagle. Metallic thread and variegated silk floss define each wisp of feather, and a glass insert for the eye contributes to the illusionistic effect.

lyre of purest classical design studded with the thirteen stars set precisely in the order in which the thirteen appear in the constellation Lyra. The conception is traditionally attributed to the elder John Adams, who is said to have advised this arrangement of the stars for the first national flag.

That the eagle flag had, by the mid-nineteenth century, come to indicate a combination of military and civilian power is confirmed by what is probably the best known of all eagle flags, that raised by "the Pathfinder of the West," John C. Frémont, on the crest of the Rocky Mountains during his first explorations in 1842. Because it was known that he would enter territory beyond our national boundaries, Frémont was not to be allowed to carry the Stars and Stripes. His bride, Jessie Benton Frémont, solved the problem in a manner harking back to the ancient tradition of regimental flags that incorporated the *elements* of the national flag, though in a clearly distinctive fashion. She designed, and then personally made, a truly brilliant interpretation by that plan (detail, page 82). Beautiful in design, the flag had, notably, a unique motif: to be more intelligible to the Indians, for whom the message was intended (for in respect to Spain Frémont was no messenger of peace), the eagle holds in one talon a peace pipe, or "calumet," in place of the traditional olive branch.

It has been suggested that, in contrast to the so-called "standards of the eagle," which were unquestionably official, eagle flags were purely personal flags not furnished by the War Department. They were, however, very much in evidence during the Mexican War as regimental flags (page 93). Furthermore, one of the oldest of all eagle flags was as "official" as possible: the Revenue Cutters Flag, now the Coast Guard and Customs Flag, which was created by act of Congress in 1799. Its precise elements were prescribed by Oliver Wolcott, Secretary of the Treasury: sixteen red and white vertical stripes, and the arms of the United States (*i.e.*, the Eagle with Shield) in dark blue on a white canton. Yet even here the "personal" element was by no means excluded: the unique vertical stripes never varied, but considerable latitude was tacitly allowed the designers as to placement of the stars (page 28).

During the Civil War, with patriotism at white heat and devotion to the Union more fervid than ever, an indignant reaction against the sacrilegious "War Against the Flag" brought not only a heightened reverence for the Stars and Stripes but the creation of eagle flags and "standards of the eagle" of more lively originality than ever before (page 95). But no mimic eagle of that period, painted or embroidered or tapestried, can rival the fame of a true, live regimental eagle, "Old Abe, the Battle Eagle" (page 94)—a truly remarkable animal which, one can almost believe, had as its goal to vindicate its kind against the taunts of Dr. Franklin.

Heroic "Old Abe" may not have been the first, or only, American battle eagle. A music sheet of 1846 (page 184)—"On to the Charge!" in honor of a fallen hero at the battle of Palo Alto, California—describes how *"Our eagle screamed and fann'd away/ The mist that veil'd the doubtful fray,"* in striking analogy with the recorded behavior of "Old Abe." The famous Wisconsin war eagle remains uncontested, however, as the most splendid and renowned incarnation of "the bird of Liberty."

The first contact that territory Indians had with the white man was likely to be either military or missionary, sometimes both, as the quietly inscrutable subject of this old photograph (<u>top left</u>) evidences, posing with an array of Stars and Stripes and one great Bible. <u>Bottom left, top right, and bottom right</u>: the themes of the flag and the eagle are echoed, together, in two examples of Mohawk Indian beadwork done at the turn of the century and by an elkskin Alaskan pillow, made during the Klondike gold rush of 1896 (which is adorned, in addition, with native flowers, especially the sky-blue blossoms of the forget-me-not). Stylistic differences in the two tribal interpretations are as vast as their geographic distances from one another. Autonomous Indian art has received much recognition recently, but perhaps sufficient attention has not been paid to the complex hybrid productions, like these, which involve the "translation" of the white man's symbols into Indian visual idiom.

The Starry Flower

The average American, if flag-conscious, recognizes the so-called Betsy Ross "wreath" of thirteen stars, the forty-eight-star flag under which most of us were born, and the current banner of half a hundred stars; he may also have some acquaintance with the renowned Star-Spangled Banner of fifteen stars and fifteen stripes on which his national anthem was based. Few Americans are aware of the once-illustrious "Great Star," perhaps the most beautiful and most loved of any Stars and Stripes. In this splendid form, the "starry flower of Liberty" —as the flag was named by Oliver Wendell Holmes—held sway during the era of national expansion: 1818 to the end of the Civil War. The Yankee Aesculapius and wit was nine years old when the first "Great Star" flag came into general national use. In his native New England it was seen more profusely than elsewhere, for it became, particularly, the flag of the American merchant marine. Suddenly blossoming all about him, the lively new banner with its assemblage of white stars into one great multi-petaled shape appeared to the child's

Detail of the canton of a thirty-four-star Civil War "Great Star" made by "Mrs. Perry." The flag was later presented to General John J. Pershing of World War I fame.

unprejudiced eye a flower rather than an abstract stellar ideograph. Displayed, worn, saluted, cheered over land and sea with respect and affection—for a longer time than any other form of Stars and Stripes—the "Great Star" has, paradoxically, been looked on by purist historians as "not official" and has been excluded from their studies, even though official guidelines for the precise design of the American flag were not set down until the second decade of the twentieth century. The neglect seems particularly absurd considering that the designer of the "Third Flag" was chosen by Congress and the flag was later officially displayed atop the Capitol.

In suggesting that the stars of the new twenty-star flag be arranged in the shape of a "Great Star," Captain Reid was not innovating. The "Great Star" pattern boasted venerable antecedents. One of the earliest motifs of American herqldry, in 1782 it appeared on the Great Seal of the United States. It also served, then, in a secondary official capacity as an elegant seal, about one inch in height, for the exclusive use of the President of Congress. To this day a "Great Star" adorns the reverse side of the one dollar bill, set above the reproduction of the Great Seal's eagle and national motto.

Popular enthusiasm over the seal had seen its elements freely adapted for patriotic decoration of objects of daily use. Familiarity with the "Great Star" pattern was therefore perhaps the reason why no visual record was made of the raising of the twenty-star flag. As neither the original flag nor the "pasteboard plan" earlier submitted has survived, the exact appearance of the memorable "Great Star" flag is a matter of conjecture. It is generally shown in reconstruction as a five-pointed star outlined by the twenty small component stars, also five-pointed. This is the least likely form it might have assumed. It is more logical to see the "Great Star" as a rather close interpretation of that on the Great Seal, its outline six-pointed. In this guise the "Great Star" was depicted in 1835 by an anonymous New England artist, who placed the great swirling national flag, grasped by an eagle, above a fluttering array of colorful pennants of all the Salem shipping houses. More significantly, in 1852 a six-pointed "Great Star" flag was selected as the sole representation of the current national standard in the first work devoted to the history of the American flag, *A History of the National Flag of the United States of America.*

Instigated by Daniel Webster and carried out on orders from General Winfield Scott by Captain (later General) Schuyler Hamilton, the publication's Plate III shows the six-pointer composed of five-pointed stars to the then-valid number of thirty. The contradiction in the use of five-pointed stars to form a six-pointed star shape is no more puzzling than the simultaneous appearance of five- and six-pointed "Great Stars," the matter being left to personal preference. One might hazard that the six-pointed pattern was traditional—and as such favored by the military—whereas the five-pointed shape represented a modern, or "liberal," point of view.

Among the number of good reasons for the appeal of the "Great Star" design was that it came closer than any other pattern to the spirit of the Flag Resolution. Its instructions had suggested the group of stars

Differing as much from geometric "Great Stars"—abstract but static—as from poetic but earthbound "Great Flowers" (see page 108), the "Great Star" below is uniquely kinetic. Five satellites revolve in measured orbit about a central ring of eight fixed—or at least slower-paced— stars. Its suggestion of movement inescapable, this deceptively simple conception comes perhaps closest of all to a visualization of the difficult goal set forth in the Flag Resolution: "…13 stars…representing a new constellation." This effect would have been impossible had not the stars still been "free"—the practice of pointing all stars in the canton in the same direction was thought of (and made mandatory) only much later.

The brilliant, silken "Great Star" flag on the opposite page and its cotton country cousin, above, have unions of twenty-six stars arranged in similar centrifugal patterns. In the former, the stars are smallest at the five angles of the "Great Star"; in the latter, the stars diminish from largest at center to smallest at the "Great Star's" tips. The design of the latter flag is also appreciably denser, a form transitional between "Great Star" and "pentagon" (page 104). Its printing—shiny on the front (shown here) and flat on the back—as well as a period repair indicate that the flag was to be flown and seen as here, with the canton on the flag's own left, contrary to present usage but frequent for antique Stars and Stripes.

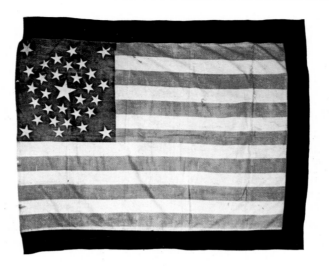

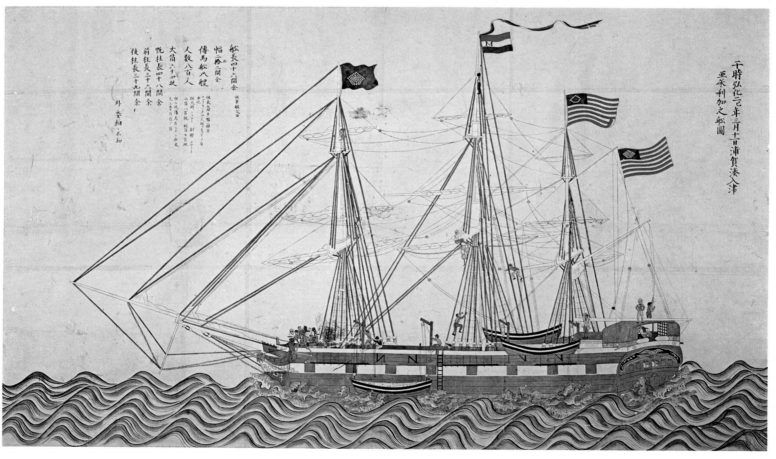

At a time when unfamiliarity blurred Oriental depictions of Western life, this apparently fanciful rendering (bottom) by a Japanese artist of an American ship's flags was based on sober fact — not inspired, as one might think, by the favorite Japanese motif of the morning glory with its pentagonal calyx. Actual "pentagon" flags and jacks existed — a natural development of the "Great Star" pattern. Top: a mid-nineteenth-century "pentagon" flag.

as "representing a new constellation." An asymmetric, fanciful arrangement—such as John Adams's proposed "Lyra Flag"—was out of the question, if only for practical reasons: how to choose or create such a pattern and, once established, the difficulties in regulating its reproduction. Admittedly, heavenly constellations did not group themselves in "Great Star" formations, but the principle of union was assuredly better symbolized by such a self-contained design than by a grid of independent rows, or ranks. Concern had been growing, too, that the stars, like the stripes, must decrease in size as they grew in number, and would lose their identity; many felt that an all-inclusive star shape would salvage the stellar symbolism and keep the composition of the flag basically unchanged regardless of the addition of stars representing new states.

The "wreath" pattern offered similar possibilities for unlimited enlargement without damage to the fundamental design and with a feeling of union. In time, however, the reduction in size of the individual stars would have reduced the pattern to a white ring on a blue ground; only at close quarters could the star symbolism have been seen. In later variations of the flag this problem was overcome by doubling or even tripling the wreath and by placing additional stars at the center and in the corners of the canton (page 161). These flags, which might be termed "medallion" flags—a name not unsuited to the formal elegance and sophistication of their designs—have been as studiously ignored by flag historians as the "Great Stars." The great "medallions" are truly that in every sense. Frequently outsized, they feature remarkably well-balanced composition and are worthy of the heroic scale and Olympian slogans they often carry. In tune with the increasingly florid taste of the Victorian Era, "medallion" patterns of truly neo-baroque magnificence were being created by about the time of the First Centennial (pages 118 and 213).

Before the stringent flag laws of the twentieth century dealt the death blow to all originality in American flag design, some daringly independent souls, unwilling to be satisfied even with personal variations on the "Great Star," "wreath," and "medallion" themes, developed patterns of what might be called "greater mobility." Their maverick designs, otherwise unclassifiable because unique, might be grouped as "kinetic," for they are kindred in their mood of high adventure and unfettered freedom (pages 114–117).

A final return to what might be called the classical style of American heraldry was attempted in the first decade of this century by Wayne Whipple, best known as the author of popular works on American history. His design for the new forty-eight-star flag was an arresting, if somewhat "androgynous," fusion of the "Great Star" and "medallion" patterns. Chosen the winner out of five hundred plans submitted, approved by President William Howard Taft, widely publicized throughout the nation, and actually produced (page 112), the Wipple Flag inexplicably fell into disuse. Silently and inexorably, the "phalanx" flag, with its serried ranks, had won the field and the last of the "Great Stars" had set.

America!

East meets West in two interpretations of the Stars and Stripes, far removed in time and space but surprisingly kindred in mood (<u>opposite page</u>, <u>left and top right</u>). An English artist's floral conception, <u>c</u>. 1800, of "the flowery banner" of the erstwhile colonies is faithfully echoed by the Japanese painter who, in 1853, showed the canton of the great flag borne by Commodore Matthew C. Perry's ship in Yedo Bay similarly spangled with four-petaled white blossoms. <u>Bottom</u>: the drama of the American flag's contrasting stripes was the focus of another Nipponese artist, who reduced the blue canton to an absolute minimum and its stars to a scattering of flowerlike white marks—a sort of "nosegay" atop the tall staff. As was the case in the United States' first contact with China (1784), Japan in the mid-nineteenth century was unfamiliar with our geometric star symbol and translated it instead into a flower shape.

"Beautiful as a flower to those who love it, terrible as a meteor to those who hate it"—thus an American orator, in 1878, extolled the flag of his country. To illustrate the first mood, one could wish no better example than this serenely beautiful flag of thirty-four stars (<u>opposite page</u>), made in 1861. Indeed a "Great Flower" rather than "Great Star," its ogival arms gently curve petal-like. The colors are appropriately soft—the luminous blue is especially notable—and the weave of the lustrous cashmere wool is so fine as to be transparent.

On another great flag of the Civil War era (<u>right</u>), also of thirty-four stars, five bold clusters of full-blown stars rest like great white blossoms or magnified snow crystals. The five independent groups are placed to form a Cross of St. Andrew, while four single stars set midway along each side of the canton clearly suggest the Cross of St. George. A thinly veiled avowal of enduring attachment to the Mother Country is perhaps indicated by the choice of the dark "navy" blue of the British flag for the blue of the American canton. (Specific regulations about tints for the American flag were not established until the twentieth century.)

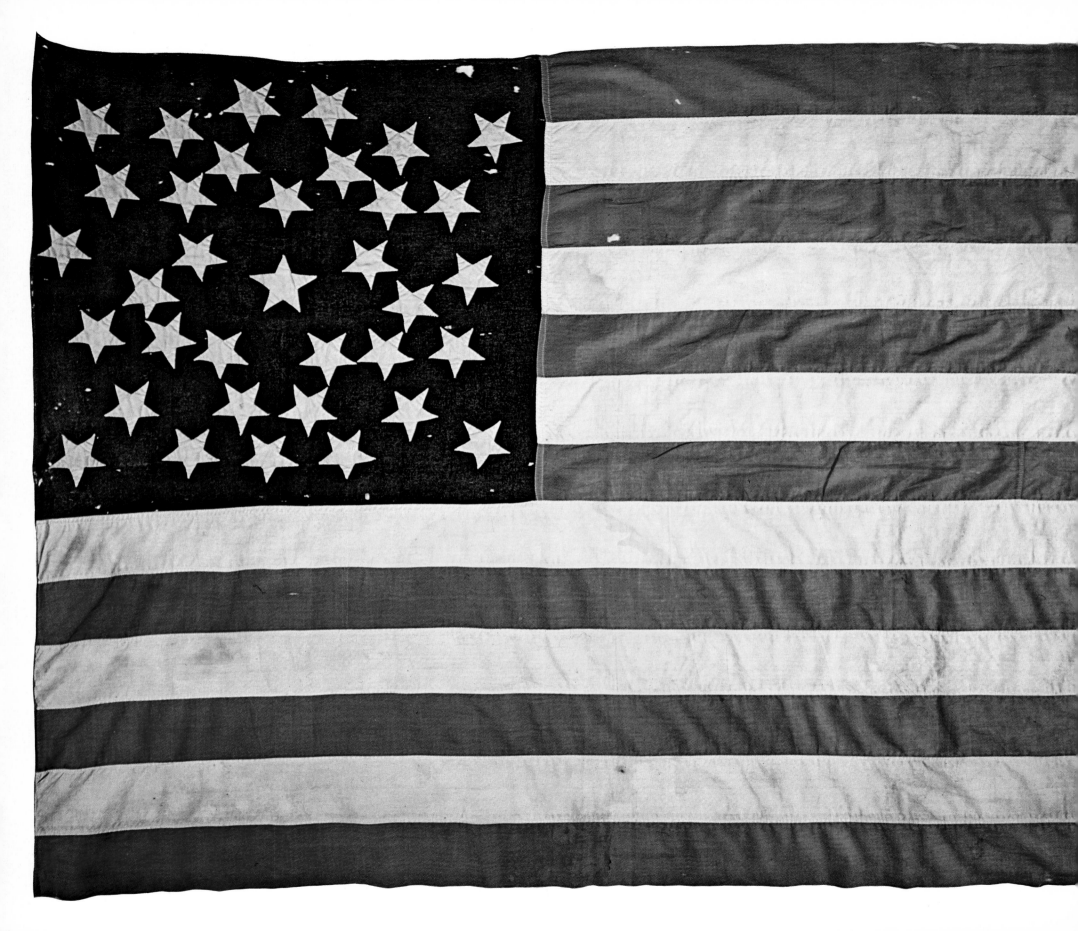

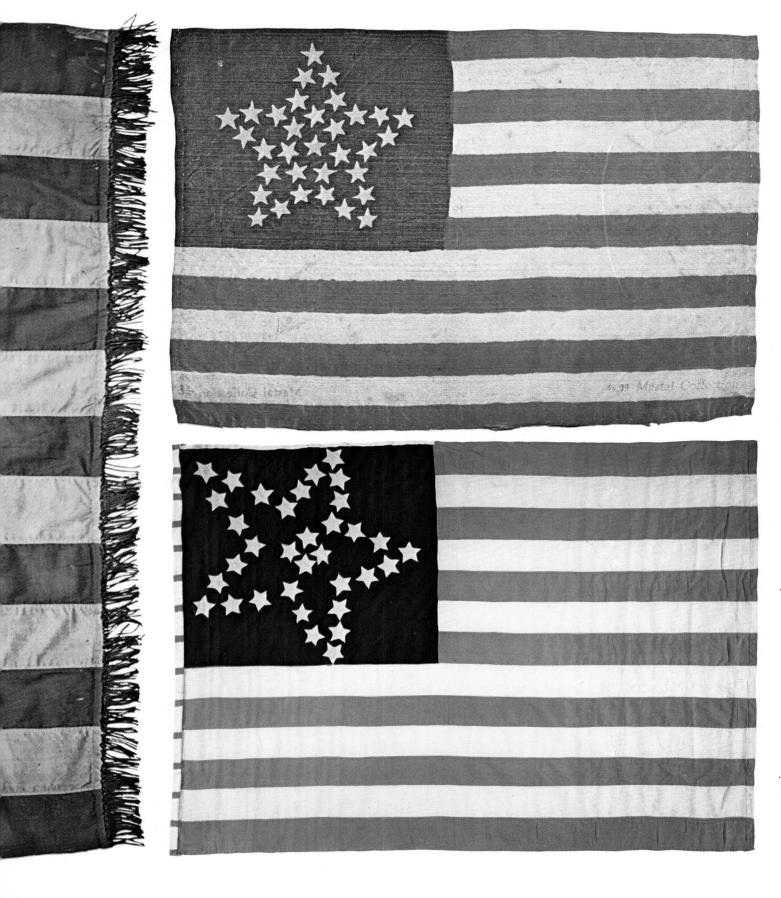

A camouflaged "Great Star" (<u>opposite page</u>). The severely geometric star shape is hidden deep within the apparently haphazard constellation of thirty-five stars in the canton. An uninhibited original variation, dating from 1863, it has indisputable kinetic elements.

The brilliantly blue canton cf a small silk flag made in 1859 (<u>top</u>) holds a delicate raceme of thirty-three stars. <u>Bottom</u>: Five asymmetric petal shapes loop out from the off-center heart of a graceful "Great Flower" pattern of thirty-four stars (1861). The candy-stripe band at left adds a whimsical touch.

The Diamond Pattern

This flag of "diamond" pattern (<u>bottom, and detail opposite page</u>) is inscribed on its headband "William Neill Irvine" (grandson of Revolutionary general William Irvine), to whom it was presented in 1855 by "his friend, Sarah Downey" of Philadelphia. The Irvine Flag consisted originally of twenty-nine stars, valid in 1847; four stars were added later. The first two were inserted, without spoiling the design, on the hoist side of the "diamond"; they correspond closely in texture and workmanship with the original twenty-nine. Indeed, a total of thirty-one stars would have been proper in 1855. The other two stars, placed haphazardly in the lower-right corner of the canton and less carefully appliquéd, must have been added, as called for, in 1858 and 1859. To reveal the beautiful original pattern, the four additional stars have been darkened in the illustration below. The Irvine Flag antedates the famed flags Sumter, also of the "diamond" pattern but "born" with their totals of thirty-three stars.

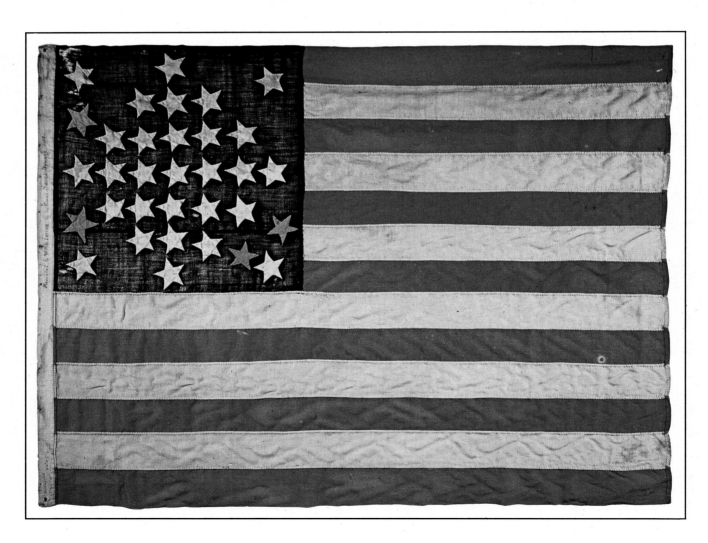

Presented to Wm N. Irvine by his friend Sarah Downey 1855.

The great "Gildersleeve Meteor"—for so this extraordinary elongated constellation of twenty-six stars might be described—carries its original owner's name, S. Gildersleeve of Connecticut. Attempts have been made to explain its pattern: some have believed it a spread-eagle human figure; others, a "Great Star," with two arms lengthened and three foreshortened; still others, the Masonic symbolic device of a compass. It is perhaps the most original interpretation of the Flag Resolution: the "new constellation" rushes headlong into space, trailing its "stars of glory."

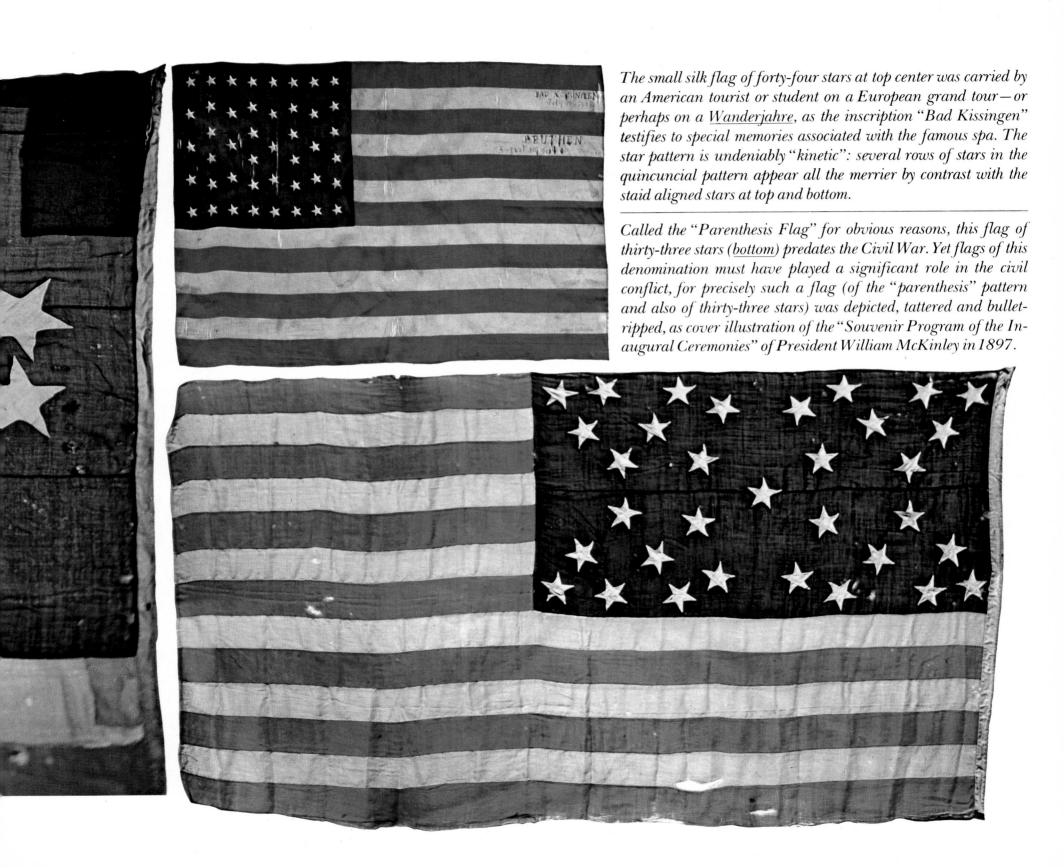

The small silk flag of forty-four stars at top center was carried by an American tourist or student on a European grand tour—or perhaps on a <u>Wanderjahre</u>, as the inscription "Bad Kissingen" testifies to special memories associated with the famous spa. The star pattern is undeniably "kinetic": several rows of stars in the quincuncial pattern appear all the merrier by contrast with the staid aligned stars at top and bottom.

Called the "Parenthesis Flag" for obvious reasons, this flag of thirty-three stars (<u>bottom</u>) predates the Civil War. Yet flags of this denomination must have played a significant role in the civil conflict, for precisely such a flag (of the "parenthesis" pattern and also of thirty-three stars) was depicted, tattered and bullet-ripped, as cover illustration of the "Souvenir Program of the Inaugural Ceremonies" of President William McKinley in 1897.

This dramatic and unorthodox First Centennial interpretation of the Stars and Stripes of thirty-seven stars (top) proclaims, in all likelihood, the designer's attachment to the South as a part of the reconstructed Union: hence, the canton's bold saltire, or Cross of St. Andrew. (The origin of the word "saltire" is the Latin salto, to leap; and, indeed, one line of stars does seem to leap over the other.) The whimsical arrangement of the balance of the stars suggests a stream of grains of sand dropping endlessly into the lower half of an hour-glass. Opposite page: the "Windblown Flag" of thirty-six stars was once the cherished possession of a Frenchman, Louis Bernard, a veteran of the Civil War and, later, a pioneer in Oregon. One wonders if he may have inspired the canton's illusionistic design, which tapers at one end, giving the impression that the flag is in motion — or "windblown" — even when at rest.

The great "medallion" flag of thirty-seven stars on the opposite page undoubtedly represents the summit of American flag designing and flagmaking. The true artist who designed it blended grace, dignity, and historic significance in perfect accord. Classically simple and effortlessly majestic, the "double-wreath" of the "medallion" has an inner ring of thirteen stars symbolizing the original Union and an outer ring of twenty-four representing the states which had been admitted to statehood since. <u>Top</u>: the original owner of this imposing flag of thirty-four stars was Thomas Cockley, who came from Ireland to Kansas in the mid-nineteenth century. The large star at the canton's center stands for his adopted state, which was admitted to the Union on July 4, 1861. The star pattern is an interesting transitional form between the "square formation" of earlier days and the true "medallion" type.

An extraordinarily beautiful flag of thirty-three stars (<u>opposite page</u>) was carried on their Westward trek by a pioneer family named Dodge. It is believed that the flag was planned before their departure and made during the long trip. Whatever dyes were at hand had to be used, and this accounts for the unusual coloring: teal blue in the canton and deep burgundy for the stripes (now turned almost brown). The pattern of stars is symmetric to the last detail, but monotony has been avoided by the felicitous use of both large and small stars. A veritable visual fugue. <u>Top</u>: the Whipple Flag of forty-eight stars—so called now after its designer Wayne Whipple, who planned to call it the "Peace Flag" (see page 232)—achieves its beauty almost as an afterthought. The primary purpose of its designer was to epitomize American history by the same technique used in the "medallion" flag on page 118, though with more complexity. Here, a central six-pointed "Great Star" symbolizes the thirteen original states, recalling both the Great Seal and the "Great Star" pattern of many early flags. The ring of stars around the "Great Star" represents the states admitted to the Union up to the time of the First Centennial. An outer ring—with space for future additions—symbolizes the states admitted since the Centennial.

IN MEMORY OF OUR DEAR PRESIDENT

Stars in the Storm

The tragic interlude of the Civil War cuts a chasm across American history. On one side, the golden period of youth comes to an abrupt halt; on the other, the modern era begins. It would be strange, indeed, if the events that wrought so profound a change had not left a mark also on the design of the flag: the preference of Civil War flagmakers was clearly for horizontal and vertical alignment of stars; that is, complete parallelism of rows, a formula that had already served some of the early Stars and Stripes (see the "Third Flag," pages 54-55). The collective visual effect of Civil War flags is, therefore, one of hypnotic rhythm—the embattled stars, drawn up in military order in defense of the threatened Union, stride on relentlessly. Star patterns of this sort, denser now and necessarily smaller, may be described as "phalanx" or "battalion" arrangements. The latter term, since it is still in modern military use, may be a less satisfactory choice for what is intended as purely graphic definition, but the period's martial mood contributed to the esteem in which such designs were held.

Detail, greatly enlarged, of a commemorative belt buckle produced for the funeral of President Abraham Lincoln (see page 154).

What is most notable in flags of this period is that, whereas emphasis was placed on regularity and geometric balance and repetition, this by no means produced monotony. Much of the work was still done by hand, even for factory flags—particularly and fortunately, the application of the stars. Machine work was restricted to the long, straight seams of the stripes. Nor, happily, was there as yet any need to follow exacting specifications of shape, size, or precise coloring, such as would be issued later, in stringent flag laws of the twentieth century. But while Civil War flags escaped much of the mortal rigidity of mechanical mass production, their artistic merit was more particularly due to the delicate design relationship of the elements and to numerous subtle details—such as the directions of the arms of the stars, which are never entirely regimented, as they are on modern flags. And truly no modern replica can either do justice to the artistic character, or render the "patina," of one of these antique flags. They are American beauties of which it may very literally be said that *"one shade the more, one ray the less"* would not only *"half-efface"* but would, in fact, entirely do away with the native *"nameless grace."*

While in the North the Stars and Stripes waxed stronger and brighter, phoenix-like in the glow of a revitalized patriotism, the Confederacy had realized the need for a flag of its own. Yet, except for a few hotheads, Southerners were as deeply attached to "the old flag" of their fathers and forefathers as were their erstwhile Northern brethren. And well they might be: Jefferson Davis, born in 1808, was the son of a soldier of the War of Independence; the son of Captain Samuel Reid, designer of the flag of twenty stars and thirteen stripes of 1818, was in the Confederate navy. To the modern mind the Great Rebellion of the 1860's is immeasurably removed from the age of the Founding Fathers. Admiral George Henry Preble, however, who fought on the side of the North as a young officer, well remembered having been presented, as a small child, to the great American painter Gilbert Stuart, first of our Old Masters and the portraitist, from life, of George Washington.

The North readily conceded that the Southern states were entitled to their share of the Stars and Stripes. This is curiously illustrated by a suggestion put forth prior to the outbreak of the conflict by no less a figure than Samuel F. B. Morse, inventor of the telegraph. Morse envisioned twin federations of American states sharing the national flag equally: the North to take half of the canton, diagonally cut across, and the upper stripes; the South, the other half of the canton, with the balance of the stripes. The moieties, hopefully, would come together once again at some future date. Such "peace flags" were flown in the North as well as in the South. In Massachusetts, however, men were tarred and feathered for the outrage.

The last Stars and Stripes was raised in the South, at New Orleans, on Washington's birthday, in February 1861. A large flag, it bore the inscription UNITED WE STAND, DIVIDED WE FALL under two clasped hands. A crowd of secessionists moved to take down the flag, but hundreds of armed men assembled, vowing to keep "the old flag" flying until nightfall, "when it was voluntarily taken down." To the people of the South—who knew that soon they must create their own banner—it was poor consolation, to be reminded by a Southern orator that "the battles of the Revolution, about which our fondest and proudest memories clus-

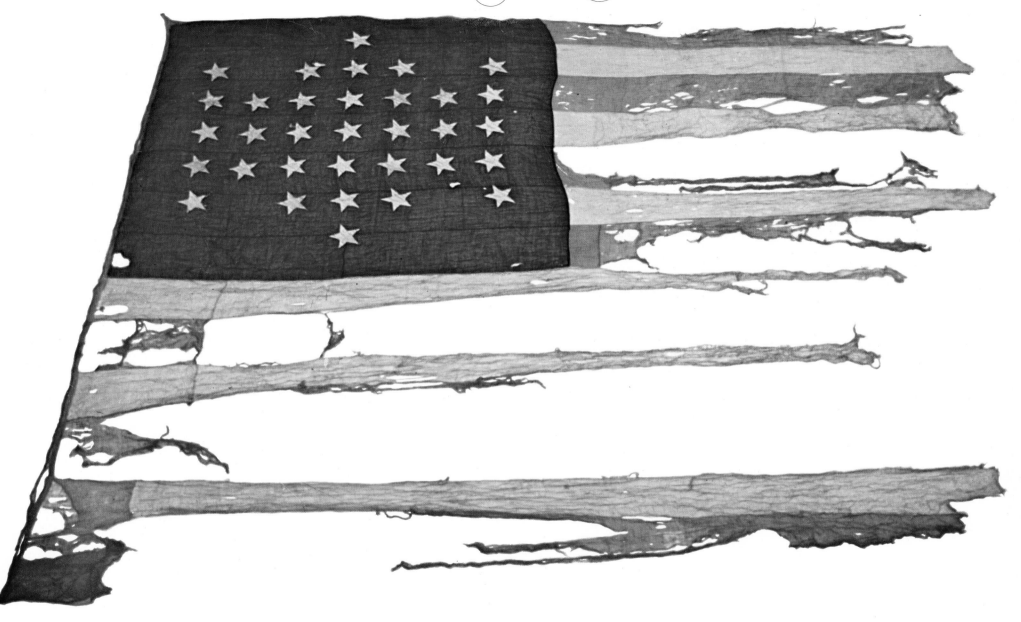

Of the two Stars and Stripes at Fort Sumter at the time of its bombardment by Southern forces, April 12 and 13, 1861, it is believed that it was this garrison flag which floated over the besieged stronghold. Taken away by the small troop of defenders when they retreated with honor, the flag was later displayed before large crowds, inspiring great indignation and enthusiasm in support of the Union. The resolve that the outraged relic would be reinstated was indeed carried out four years later. But on that same day, April 14, 1865, tragedy walked on the heels of triumph: Lincoln fell under the bullets of John Wilkes Booth. The flag's design is a truly beautiful variation of the traditional—though rare—pattern of the "cross," or "diamond" (seen before in the earlier Irvine Flag, pages 112–113, and in the Hulbert Flag of thirteen stars, page 34).

The Flag of Union

The unusual length of the field of the great Civil War flag of thirty-four stars below indicates that it was probably a naval flag. Despite minor irregularities, the pattern in the canton is basically a square "phalanx" of thirty stars in five aligned parallel rows of six stars each, with two independent "leaders" on the fly (or outer) side of the canton and two "stragglers" on the hoist side (next to the staff). That the "Great Star" pattern nevertheless continued to be used simultaneously with the favored "phalanx" is evidenced in a picture (*opposite page, bottom right*) from FRANK LESLIE'S ILLUSTRATED HISTORY OF THE CIVIL WAR *showing "The Sixth Regiment of Massachusetts Volunteers Leaving Jersey City Railroad Depot to Defend Washington, D.C., April 18th, 1861."* Opposite page, top left, center, and right: *three expressions of Northern indignation against the Southern rebellion, branded as "The War Against the Flag" — the Dix token coin, commemorating the famous order of General John Adams Dix, January 29, 1861: "If anyone attempts to haul down the American flag, shoot him on the spot"; a certificate of membership to the ladies' division of a patriotic organization (by Currier & Ives, its vignettes highlight the all-pervasiveness of the flag in American women's lives); a patriotic song sheet by the renowned New York publisher Charles Magnus, with words by the Rev. J. P. Lundy to the tune of "Woodsman, Spare That Tree."*

It is seldom possible to pinpoint the date of execution of a flag as closely as it is this one. Because its canton rests on the "war stripe," this thirty-three-star flag was in all probability made after the start of hostilities on April 12, 1861, but before the flag of thirty-four stars became official on July 4—Kansas having been admitted to the Union in January of that year. Not only does the flag revive the "war stripe" tradition but its placement of stars in a lively, unregimented, "scatter" pattern also harks back to earlier days. Opposite page: in contrast, this large flag, 22 feet long by 16 feet wide, achieves perfect symmetry in its horizontally and vertically aligned stars. The coloring of still-brilliant ultramarine blue and somewhat faded carmine, as well as the texture of mixed fibers, is characteristic of other flags of the period of New England origin. The stars are double-appliquéd by hand, but this outsized flag may have been made at a New England factory—perhaps in Saxonville, Massachusetts, where the production of American bunting—to replace imported Yorkshire bunting—was first attempted in 1837.

ter, were not [yet] fought beneath the folds of the stars and stripes." Not surprisingly therefore, when the choice of a flag for the South was made the subject of a contest, and hundreds of entries were submitted, the designs which retained both the devices and colors of the Stars and Stripes were favored above all others. Many of these were excellent (pages 136–137), but the palm was eventually awarded to a design which would become known as the "Stars and Bars" (page 134) and which not merely incorporated the stars and the stripes but reverted to the old "wreath" pattern—of seven stars at first, then eleven.

The "Stars and Bars" was the first national flag of the Confederacy. Earlier Southern banners had included the "Palmetto Flag," the "Bonnie Blue Flag," and the "Pelican Flag"; these may be compared to the "Pine Tree Flag," the "Rattlesnake Flag," and other predecessors of the Stars and Stripes. It was, paradoxically, the new Southern flag's strong family resemblance to the Stars and Stripes that brought about its demise early in the war. From the start, it proved confusing in battle, and the two sides exchanged accusations of using the adversary's flag. Within six months, therefore, the "Stars and Bars" was replaced by the "Southern Cross" (page 136), most renowned in a squared version, as the "Battle Flag" of the Confederacy. Unlike the "Stars and Bars," the "Southern Cross" bore no evident relationship to the Union flag (one tenuous link is the use of thirteen symbolic stars spaced along the saltire, or Cross of St. Andrew—although the Confederate states never officially numbered more than eleven). The new flag, under either of its several forms (page 141), is today often referred to as "The Conquered Banner" or "The Flag of the Lost Cause." These sad titles might apply better to the "Stars and Bars," which has indeed largely faded away; the "Southern Cross" has, by contrast, continued to lead an active career as unofficial regional banner of the Southland and has been incorporated as an element in no less than five Southern state flags.

The significant and final triumph, of course, was the Stars and Stripes'. Beyond the strong patterns it developed (the valorous, robust "phalanx") and the tangential offspring it sired (the "Stars and Bars"), the cult of the national flag, as it has endured to this day, was a direct outcome of the Great Rebellion. Indeed, that conflict has been called—by Admiral Preble, the flag's premier historian—"the War Against the Flag and the Union." Moreover, the concept of union was, as a British historian put it, "the idol of every American heart," and therefore so also was union's sacred emblem, the flag. In precisely such terms, orator and statesman Edward Everett, in Boston two weeks after the attack on Fort Sumter, spoke of "the flag, always honored, always beloved [but now] worshipped." The word was by no means too strong. And what had been a stern and solemn enthusiasm in wartime became a joyous delirium at war's conclusion. As one writer asserted: "After the fall of Sumter [to Federal troops] Cincinnati was fairly iridescent with the red, white and blue." Cincinnati was but typical of all cities, towns, and villages over the length and breadth of the land.

As is enthusiasm's way, the "flag fever" of the Civil War period ran to extremes, even extended literally from the minute to the gigantic: a patriotic needlewoman would keep her tools covered prettily by a dainty, silk-lined tapestry flag (page 176), and the very needles themselves would serve to make the outsized flags

The Phalanx Pattern

The strikingly original "Open-Center Flag" of thirty-four stars recalls the "square formation" pattern of earlier days (pages 45, 77, and 78), but the purpose of the arrangement may have been primarily practical, space being allowed for the thirty-fifth star (West Virginia's), known to be shortly forthcoming. If so, the maker also showed considerable ingenuity, as well as a charming courtliness, in reserving for the newcomer the central position. The patterning made possible the balanced design of equal, aligned rows, the sturdy "phalanx" apparently facing attack staunchly in all directions. In addition, however—and the remark applies to all these antique American flags—since no attention was paid to matching the directions of the stars' rays, and other minor irregularities are evident in the handwork, there is a pleasant sparkle that preserves the composition from ponderousness.

Although the flag of thirty-six stars, including Nevada, could not become official until the prescribed date, Independence Day, 1865, the new flag was made and flown well in advance. In times of such dire trial, the newest member would not be made to wait for its place in the family circle. Few flags would have been more worthy to preside over the soon-to-come peace celebrations than this serenely beautiful star pattern that achieves an effect of lightness and luminosity through the use of the airy quincuncial formation. The strong diagonal structure suggests the pattern of the present-day flag, although here the individual stars, fewer in number, are considerably larger.

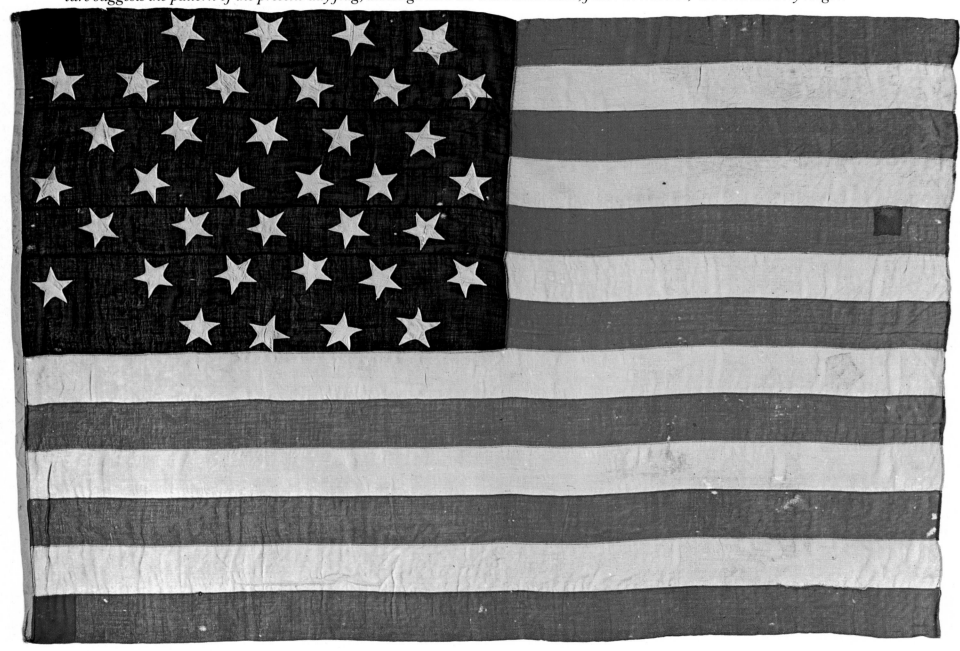

for which "flag bees" were sometimes assembled. On one large Stars and Stripes, the Newcomb Flag, four generations of a family toiled—the great-grandmother recalling, while at work, her memories of childhood during the War of 1812. An even larger force must have cooperated in the making of "a well-proportioned national flag, ninety feet in length," which was flown atop the spire of the Roman Catholic cathedral in patriotic Cincinnati—on that joyous occasion of the fall of Fort Sumter to a victorious North. It is more surprising to learn, from an eyewitness, that on the occupation of Richmond by Federal troops, April 3, 1865, "a multitude of little U.S. flags…hundreds of them, not more than a foot long, and many wrought on silk were fluttering along the streets."

In 1866, one year after the Northern victory, the State of Iowa proudly declared: "The State has no State flag other than the stars and stripes, a large interest in which she claims." Brigham Young concurred, for Utah: "We have no territorial flag. Our flag is the flag of the nation—the stars and stripes."

In that same year was flown what was called, startlingly, "the first real American flag." Justification for the description is that all flag bunting previous to that time had been made in Yorkshire, England (although flags of other material, made in America, had been produced). Experiments in weaving bunting had been carried out as early as 1837 at the New England Worsted Company, of Saxonville, Massachusetts, but this native material was not judged suitable for flag use. In 1865, however, General Benjamin F. Butler, the so-called "Beast of New Orleans" (for his merciless repression of that occupied city), founded in Lowell, Massachusetts, the United States Bunting Company. On February 21, 1866, a great thirty-six-star flag made of the firm's bunting was raised over the national Capitol. It was a technical and patriotic triumph.

Whatever its texture, the flag of Union and of the victor went on not only to endure but to grow and multiply beyond any expectation. All Stars and Stripes of later periods are in the strictest sense its lineal descendants, conceived in that troubled era when, for four long years of strife, our "stars of glory" were firm beacons of hope amidst the raging storm.

THE CONFEDERACY

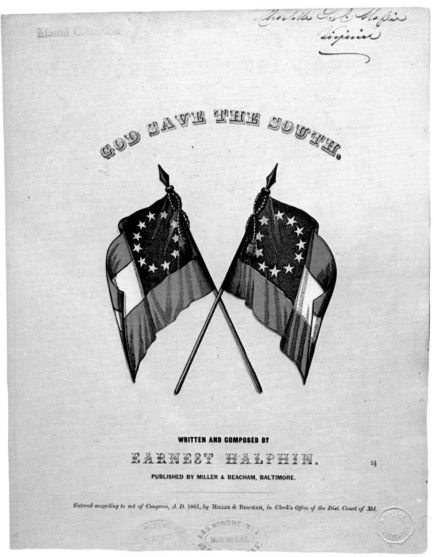

An early example, dated Savannah, May 1861, of the first flag of the South: the "Stars and Bars" (<u>opposite page</u>). The back, or reverse, is at left; the front, or obverse, at right. A detail (<u>top left</u>) shows an inscription on the reverse of the canvas headband, as well as workmanship of the stars, which were inserted in single thickness in the material of the canton. The conception of the "Stars and Bars" was clearly derived from the Stars and Stripes, the stripes being enlarged into three broad bands while seven stars (for the first seven states to secede) were displayed in the traditional "wreath" pattern. Credit for the design is generally given to a Prussian artist, Nicola Marschall, who then resided in Marion, Alabama. The first "Stars and Bars" actually flown was raised over the Southern capitol, at Montgomery, on the day of the flag's acceptance by the congress assembled there, March 4, 1861. The number of stars was finally increased to eleven — as seen in the Southern music sheet, bottom left — to represent the final number of states officially members of the Confederacy.

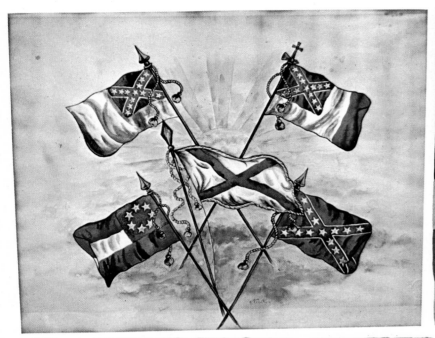 

The four Confederate flags carried in the South during the Civil War are pictured in a contemporary watercolor (opposite page, top left). Counter-clockwise, at bottom left is the "Stars and Bars"; at bottom right, the "Southern Cross," which soon succeeded it and a squared-off version of which became famous as the "Battle Flag," though it was never officially adopted as such; at upper right, the "White Man's Flag," or "Stainless Banner," with an entirely white field; and at upper left, its second, short-lived version, with the addition of a red band at the end of the field. At center is the state flag of Alabama, presumably the artist's home state. Bottom: an interesting Southern ensign, battle-worn and blood-stained, bearing eleven blue stars.

The contest organized in 1861 to select a design for a flag of the Confederacy included, according to the chairman's report, "a mass of models or designs more or less copied from the United States flag." Two representative examples—opposite page, top right, and this page, bottom left—both include a constellation of thirteen stars. The second is strongly suggestive of the saltire of the future "Southern Cross." Bottom right: genuine attachment to the symbolic first union of thirteen stars combined with a hope that the Southern federation would soon attain that total number of states. For this reason, many early "Stars and Bars" optimistically displayed, like this one (a silken miniature), thirteen stars arranged in a "wreath" of twelve stars with a thirteenth at center. Precisely the same device, except that the field contained thirteen stripes, was being used on miniature flags in the North at this time. And in both South and North, dainty "flaglets" were made for or by children; known also as "Bible flags," these were often put for safekeeping in the Great Book.

The splendid star within a wreath of ten smaller stars on the canton of this regulation "Stars and Bars" contributes greatly to the beauty of the composition. The Confederate flagmaker may well have been inspired by a memory of "the bonnie blue flag that bore a single star," the famous first Southern banner of ralliement. But in fact the use of a larger central star was for purely practical reasons: the star was known as "the Virginia star," a form of flattery meant to entice the then-still-reluctant "old Dominion" to join the Confederacy. _Opposite page:_ a unique regimental banner bears an unorthodox Confederate constellation of twelve stars, in place of the official eleven. The extra star may reasonably be taken to represent a Southern state which did not secede but which supplied many volunteers to the Confederate cause—some of them, no doubt, in this particular corps. GOD ARMETH THE PATRIOT, _the regimental motto embroidered in cross-stitch (detail) arching above the central star, had appeared in 1813 on the beautiful eagle standard of a Nashville regiment (page 89). While mottoes related in mood were used on other Confederate banners—that of "Terry's Texas Rangers" was_ GOD DEFEND THE RIGHT, _and an Alabama troop proclaimed_ OUR COUNTRY AND OUR RIGHTS—_the archaic slogan seen here may hark back beyond the Revolutionary period, perhaps having been brought to the colonies by some Puritan exile._

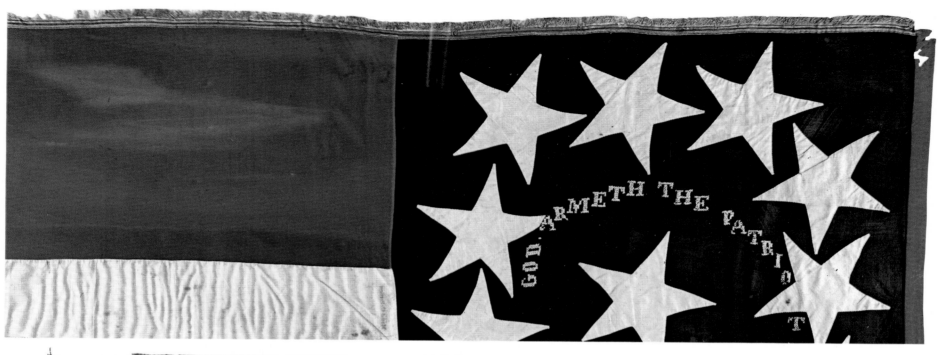

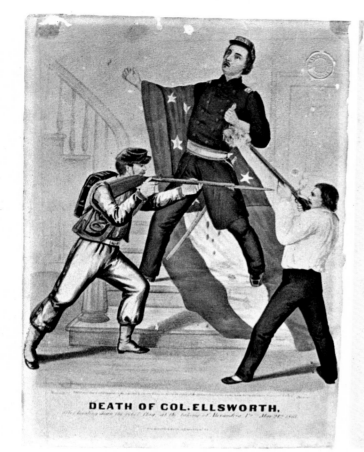

DEATH OF COL. ELLSWORTH.

ELLSWORTH
A TRIBUTE TO THE MEMORY.

OF THE LATE
COLONEL ELLSWORTH.

Two Currier & Ives lithographs (top left and center) illustrate a tragic episode of the War Between the States. Young Colonel Elmer E. Ellsworth, commander of the dashing New York Zouaves and a personal friend of the Lincoln family, was shot point-blank in Alexandria, Virginia, in May 1861, by an enraged civilian for having hauled down a Confederate flag. Simultaneously, the rebel was shot by Ellsworth's devoted aide.

An official "Stars and Bars" of seven stars, at bottom, is of unusually vivid crimson coloring. Opposite page, top left: the "White Man's Flag" was in use only during the last few months of the Civil War. The red band at its outer edge (a variant of the flag) was added to prevent its being confused with a surrender flag.

"The Confederate Flag," a poem by John Dimitry (opposite page, top right), was etched by Charles B. Hall, New York, in 1897. It pays mournful tribute to "The Flag of the Lost Cause," by then only "a glorified memory." Bottom: in South as well as North (see pages 150–151 for Union examples), patriotically ornamented envelopes were the rage. The example at left, with coiled serpent and historic motto, is a reminder that American independence came about, too, by a justified rebellion. At center and right, the portrait and signature, respectively, of President Jefferson Davis on two versions of the "Stars and Bars."

A printed flag of thirty-six stars.

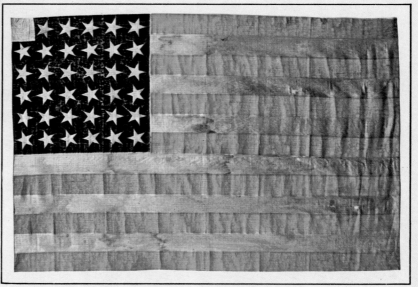

Five flags of the Civil War period. <u>Bottom of page</u>: at left, a thirty-six-star flag (one star covered) of glazed muslin; at center, an exquisite small silk flag with tall narrow canton of clear blue and embroidered white stars; at right, A PICTURE OF THE FLAG OF THE UNION, *with Hebrew inscription, Joshua I, 4 to 9, presented by Abraham Kohn, Chicago city clerk, to Lincoln on February 11, 1861.*

A thirty-five-star flag of fine wool serge, with an unusual blue band.

Five vignettes from a display (across center of pages) in HARPER'S MAGAZINE, July 4, 1864, dramatically illustrate the role of the American flag in military and in civilian life during the Civil War period.

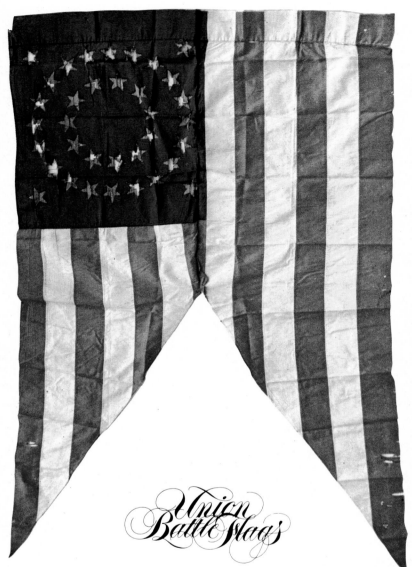

KNOXVILLE,

ATLANTA,

FRANKLIN, NASHVILLE,

WILMINGTON,

Union Battle Flags

A swallow-tailed cavalry guidon of thirty-five stars, top left, is of silk. The stars are gold-painted. *Top right:* on the national colors of the 23rd Army Corps, the stars are arranged to outline a tripartite shield. On the stripes are names of battles in which the corps participated. *Bottom right:* a picture from FRANK LESLIE'S ILLUSTRATED HISTORY OF THE CIVIL WAR shows the "Decisive Bayonet Charge by Federal Troops, Led by General Tyler, at the Battle of Winchester, Virginia, on March 23, 1862."

The pattern of this sumptuous constellation of thirty-four stars resembles that of the guidon on the opposite page, but the canton's special and most striking feature is the large capital "L" at its center, rendered with masterly sculptural relief. No clues have been found to the meaning of the letter, which may have been the initial of a place name or the Roman numeral symbol for 50 (and, by implication, 50th). Military experts have been able to furnish no information, but the museum of the West Point Academy has in its collections an unidentified thirty-four-star cavalry guidon that shows a capital "L" at the center of a starry "double-wreath," its canton, however, of the more usual dark-blue tint. Cavalry guidons with thirty-four stars on a <u>light</u>-*blue canton were produced during the Civil War but never issued to the troops.*

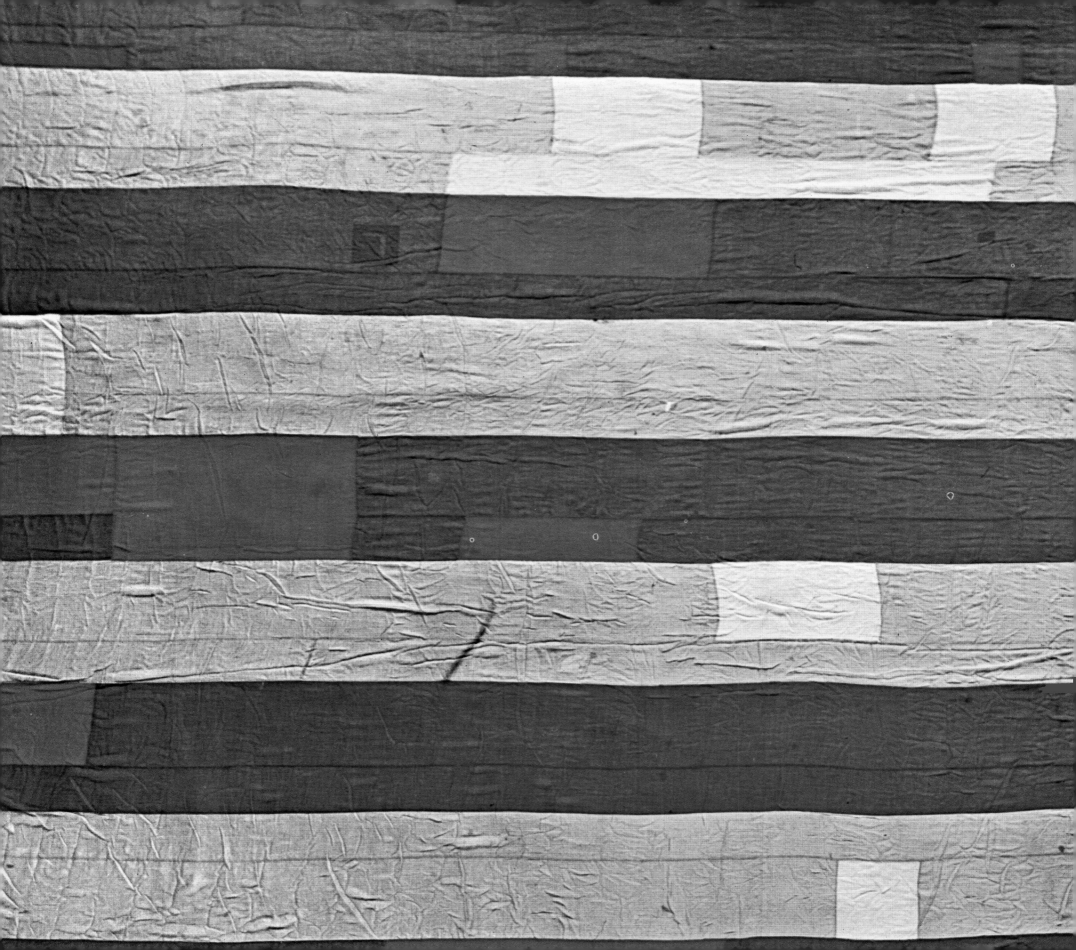

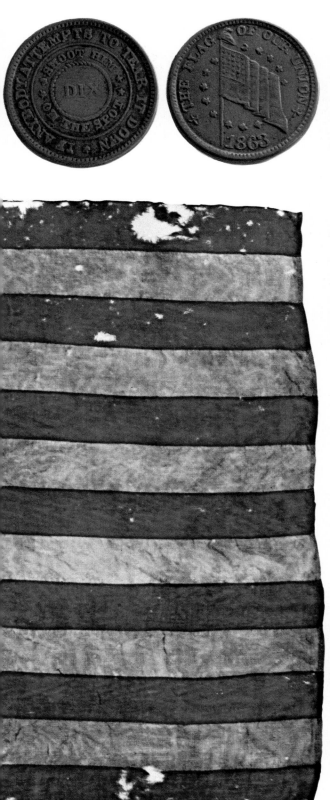

TRAITOR,
SPARE
that FLAG.

By the Rev. J. P. LUNDY.

AIR—"Woodman spare that tree."

Traitor, spare that flag,
Touch not a single star,
Its sheltering glory still,
Increaseth near and far;
'Twas our forefathers' hand,
That placed it o'er our head,
And thou shalt let it stand,
Or perish with the dead.

That dear old precious flag,
Whose glory and renown,
Are spread o'er land and sea,
And would'st thou tear it down?
Traitor, forbear thy touch,
Rend not its heart-bound ties,
Oh! spare that glorious flag,
Still streaming through the skies

When I was yet a boy,
I gloried in the sight,
And raised my voice in joy,
To greet its folds of light;
For it is my home is dear,
Dear is my native land;
Forgive this foolish tear,
But led that old flag stand.

My heart-strings round the cling,
Close as thy stripes, old friend,
Thy praises nicer shall sing,
Till time itself shall end;
Old flag, the storm still brave,
And, traitor, leave the spot,
While I've a hand to save,
Thy touch shall harm it not

Ten Illustrated Songs on Notepaper, mailed to any Address on
receipt of 50 cts. Published by Chas. Magnus, 12 Frankfort St., N. Y.

It is seldom possible to pinpoint the date of execution of a flag as closely as it is this one. Because its canton rests on the "war stripe," this thirty-three-star flag was in all probability made after the start of hostilities on April 12, 1861, but before the flag of thirty-four stars became official on July 4—Kansas having been admitted to the Union in January of that year. Not only does the flag revive the "war stripe" tradition but its placement of stars in a lively, unregimented, "scatter" pattern also harks back to earlier days. <u>Opposite page:</u> in contrast, this large flag, 22 feet long by 16 feet wide, achieves perfect symmetry in its horizontally and vertically aligned stars. The coloring of still-brilliant ultramarine blue and somewhat faded carmine, as well as the texture of mixed fibers, is characteristic of other flags of the period of New England origin. The stars are double-appliquéd by hand, but this outsized flag may have been made at a New England factory—perhaps in Saxonville, Massachusetts, where the production of American bunting—to replace imported Yorkshire bunting—was first attempted in 1837.

THE OLD FLAG OF THE WAR. 1861-5

A practice severely frowned upon by governmental authorities—and by President Lincoln in particular—was the custom indulged in by some Unionists of removing from the national constellation the number of stars equivalent to the seceded states—or even of those states whose loyalty to the Union appeared doubtful. Accordingly, the total was wont to vary. *Opposite page, top, and bottom left:* two examples, respectively, of twenty-one and twenty-three stars. The first, a maverick, has its stars in parallel vertical "rows" of alternately three and four. The second, conceived as a "double-wreath" of sorts, has a single star at center and at each corner of the canton.

Affectionately and reverently known as "the old flag," the Stars and Stripes of thirteen stars—a symbol of loyalty to the original Union—was much in use during the Civil War, both privately and by the military. *Opposite page, bottom right:* a flag flown on a whaling ship has its stars in a popular variation of the old "Third Maryland" pattern (pages 42 and 44), but is noticeably different by the use, characteristic in this later period, of a larger star at center. This pattern was a great favorite, also, with the troops. In another thirteen-star flag, at left, the stars are in a quincuncial staggered pattern. The period stenciled band was added for an exhibition of the flag after the war.

Preceding overleaf: the canton and part of the field of the largest Civil War flag known, 43 feet long by 30 feet wide—approximately the measurements of the Star-Spangled Banner in its original condition. This colossus of thirty-five stars, valid from July 4, 1863, to July 4, 1865, floated above the station of the Erie Railroad central depot in Jersey City, New Jersey, from which so many troops left for the battle lines (see also page 127).

EPISTOLARY PATRIOTISM

was rampant throughout the war period,

MAJ. GEN. GEO. B. McCLELLAN.

"What if a hungry rat should cross the path of an Elephant, squelch it, by Heaven, squelch it."

The New Quaker Bonnet. 1861.

The Country's in danger!— that's what's the matter.

and was more than adequately encouraged by publishers eager to meet the demand for a multitude of designs on envelopes and stationery. Themes ranged in mood all the way from the pathetic to the satirical; in the latter mood they often appear to be forerunners of what would, in time, become modern "cartooning."

The use of no more than four rows of stars on a correspondingly elongated canton—in place of the customary six, or at least five, rows—constituted a daring innovation in this great flag of thirty-six stars, valid for the period 1865–1867. In addition, the design was preserved from monotony, and striking originality expressed, by the simple but genial placing of the two central rows noticeably closer to each other than to the two outer rows. Certainly one of the happiest interpretations of the "phalanx" pattern, it is—like a flag of the same period shown on page 131—far less military in mood than previous treatments of the theme, and is therefore ideally suited to the postbellum mood.

A now universally famous name was coined by Captain Stephen Driver, a shipmaster of Salem, Massachusetts, in 1831. As he was leaving upon one of many world voyages— this particular one would be climaxed by the rescue of the mutineers of the BOUNTY— friends presented him with a beautiful flag of twenty-four stars. As the banner opened to the ocean breeze for the first time, he exclaimed: "Old Glory!" Many years later, the old shipmaster retired to Nashville, and during the Civil War secreted his beloved flag so well— by quilting it into his bed coverlet— that it escaped detection. At the war's end, the venerable relic was proudly raised by its owner over the Tennessee state capitol. It is the most illustrious of a number of flags— both Northern and Confederate— reputed to have similarly been hidden, then later revealed as times changed. But Captain Driver remains "godfather" to the national flag; his very personal note is the appliquéd anchor in the lower-right corner of the canton. ("Old Glory" may no longer be opened up to be photographed, and no color photograph is available.)

FRANK LESLIE'S ILLUSTRATED HISTORY OF THE CIVIL WAR *described the scene at top left as follows: "The Old Flag Again on Sumter—Raised (on a temporary staff formed of an oar and a boathook) by Captain H. M. Bragg, of General Gillmore's Staff, February 18th, 1865." The "old flag" here is a "Great Star" formed by an intersecting triangle and "arrowhead."*

To all U.S. Congressmen attending the ceremonies of the state funeral of President Lincoln were issued souvenir bronze buckles of the event, cast from the metal of Confederate cannons. <u>Top center</u>: the front and back of the buckle, whose official design—embodying a dual message of triumph and mourning—had been approved by the President's widow. <u>Right and opposite page</u>: a band of crepe surrounds a "Great Star" flag used following the assassination of the President. The band was not removed, and the flag later served for the mourning of other assassinated Presidents, including John F. Kennedy. The brilliantly sparkling "Great Star"—of thirty-six elements—is an exceedingly geometric treatment of the motif, its pattern far removed from the flowerlike, earlier "Great Stars" (pages 108 and 111). It is, in fact, a perfect pentagram.

The First Centennial

Popular interpretation of the Stars and Stripes undoubtedly reached its apogee of variety and originality at the time of the First Centennial. Since no trammels of any kind were yet placed on flagmakers' imaginations and no strict distinctions were as yet drawn between official and unofficial designs (both types ranked, justifiably, as American flags), it is no surprise that, on the occasion of the Centennial, creativeness in flag design was not the exception but the rule. The styles ranged from genuine folk art to what one must qualify as fine art. One-of-a-kind homemade examples were sometimes endearingly naïve, as is the "Four-Cornered Flag" (page 163), sometimes reflected a consummate sophistication, as does the "Hour-Glass Flag" (page 116). The masterpiece of an anonymous commercial designer (page 159; detail shown page 156) is a complex play on the number "76": the Centennial dates 1776 and 1876 are formed each of thirty-eight glittering stars (the number then valid for the flag), making a total of seventy-six. The result reflects with pyrotechnic brilliance the mood of national jubila-

The first one hundred years: detail of the dates which decorate a First Centennial flag shown in full on page 159.

A thirty-eight-star flag of simplest design was given timely significance—a Centennial salute—by the addition of word and date on two of its white stripes. The use of such extraneous devices—inscriptions, portraits, etc.—on the flag was not yet deemed reprehensible.

The First Centennial

Popular interpretation of the Stars and Stripes undoubtedly reached its apogee of variety and originality at the time of the First Centennial. Since no trammels of any kind were yet placed on flagmakers' imaginations and no strict distinctions were as yet drawn between official and unofficial designs (both types ranked, justifiably, as American flags), it is no surprise that, on the occasion of the Centennial, creativeness in flag design was not the exception but the rule. The styles ranged from genuine folk art to what one must qualify as fine art. One-of-a-kind homemade examples were sometimes endearingly naïve, as is the "Four-Cornered Flag" (page 163), sometimes reflected a consummate sophistication, as does the "Hour-Glass Flag" (page 116). The masterpiece of an anonymous commercial designer (page 159; detail shown page 156) is a complex play on the number "76": the Centennial dates 1776 and 1876 are formed each of thirty-eight glittering stars (the number then valid for the flag), making a total of seventy-six. The result reflects with pyrotechnic brilliance the mood of national jubila-

The first one hundred years: detail of the dates which decorate a First Centennial flag shown in full on page 159.

A thirty-eight-star flag of simplest design was given timely significance — a Centennial salute — by the addition of word and date on two of its white stripes. The use of such extraneous devices — inscriptions, portraits, etc. — on the flag was not yet deemed reprehensible.

A WAGON LOAD FROM JERSEY.

To American flagmakers—patriots no doubt, but businessmen also—the occasion of the Centennial presented literally a once-in-a-hundred-years challenge and taxed their imaginations to the utmost. The palm clearly must go to the anonymous creator of the dazzlingly brilliant design at bottom left.

The merry excursionists in "A Wagon Load from Jersey" (<u>top left</u>), shown in HARPER'S WEEKLY, *July 4, 1876, may well have been waving one of the many commemorative flags issued for the Centennial celebrations. Even the faithful farm horses taking the family to the Philadelphia exposition have been spruced up for the event: each sports its own "flaglet" rhythmically bobbing atop its patient head. <u>Top right</u>: this small flag counts but thirty-three stars in its "double-wreath" constellation (with four corner and one central stars). Likely it would be the banner of celebrants hailing from the thirty-third state, Oregon. Similar banners, with appropriate numbers of stars, appear to have been issued for other states during this period (see pages 172–173).*

tion. In contrast to it, the noble classicism of the great "medallion" flags (pages 118–121) is serenely timeless, transcending purely national connotations by virtue of superlative design merit.

The splendid Centennial tributes to the Stars and Stripes were tendered one year before the anniversary of the flag, which, by strict observance, should have been commemorated on June 14, 1877. Public sentiment, however, could not conceive of a national *agape* the year before which would exclude the beloved emblem. Therefore, although the Grand Union Flag—which had preceded the Stars and Stripes—was flown over the Old State House in Philadelphia on January 1, 1876, the great exposition there paid homage primarily to the national flag. The Star-Spangled Banner went on view for the first time since it had flown over Fort McHenry; also shown, less happily, was the alleged flag of the *Bonhomme Richard*, later discredited by historians. Yet, for us today, these well-intentioned flag exhibits could not possibly compare in interest with what contemporary visitors perhaps scarcely noted: an exuberant multitude of up-to-date American flags that bedecked both the exposition proper and, in varying degrees, the entire nation.

The flags of the First Centennial, beyond their individual characteristics, have an arresting peculiarity: they feature, variously, three different total numbers of stars—thirty-seven, at that time the proper number (valid until July 4, 1877, when Colorado's star would be added); thirty-eight, in honor of the imminent admission of Colorado, on August 1, 1876; or thirty-nine, because for some time it had been believed that two territories would be raised to statehood during the centennial year. Actually, a thirty-nine-star flag was never to become official—not only did the Dakotas, late in 1889, bring the total states to forty, but three other admissions (Montana, Washington, and Idaho) occurred so swiftly thereafter that the official constellation leaped in 1890, on July 4—the traditional date for inclusion of a new state in the flag—from thirty-eight to forty-three.

The advance use of the thirty-eight-star flag was promptly excused by Colorado's entry. Furthermore, there were illustrious precedents for such an infraction. The great "Third Flag" of twenty stars had been flown several months ahead of the specified date in 1818. Also, no further back than February 22, 1861, President-Elect Abraham Lincoln had with his own hands raised at Independence Hall, on his way to his inauguration, a flag of thirty-four stars. Although Kansas had become the thirty-fourth state on January 29, the number of stars should have remained officially thirty-three until July 4. The official code was superseded by the unwritten law: a newcomer to the family of states should not be kept out by mere technicality in the solemn moments either of ordeal or of rejoicing.

An English visitor observed justly, in 1820, that Americans lived in the future, "appealing not to history but to prophecy, glorying rather in the achievements of their posterity than in a long line of ancestors." There had never been better cause for confidence in the American future than in 1876. While a large part of the continent was still unsettled, it was clear that, in spite of some formidable obstacles—the tragic episode of Custer's Last Stand occurred on June 25, 1876, a few days before the centennial date—the progress of science and industry augured the prospect that the taming of the balance of the "Great American Desert"

The Flag of a Hundred Years

The Matthew McNamara Flag—so-called from the name of its original owner—is joyously exuberant in its design: a circular "double-wreath" with larger central star and triads of stars at each corner. It is a faithful reflection of the national optimism of the period, but one star too many brings it to a premature total of thirty-nine (see page 160).

The First Centennial

The "International Flag," patented in 1875 with an unofficial total of thirty-nine stars in its constellation, is notable not only for its canton—which contains six vertical "rows," three with small stars and three with large stars—but also for its border of small flags of the nations that were to attend the United States' hundredth birthday party. It brings to mind a flag carried by the printers of calico for the July 4, 1788, celebrations in Philadelphia; on that occasion the Stars and Stripes was surrounded by an edge of thirty-seven prints of various colors and carried the motto "May the Union government protect the manufacturers of America."

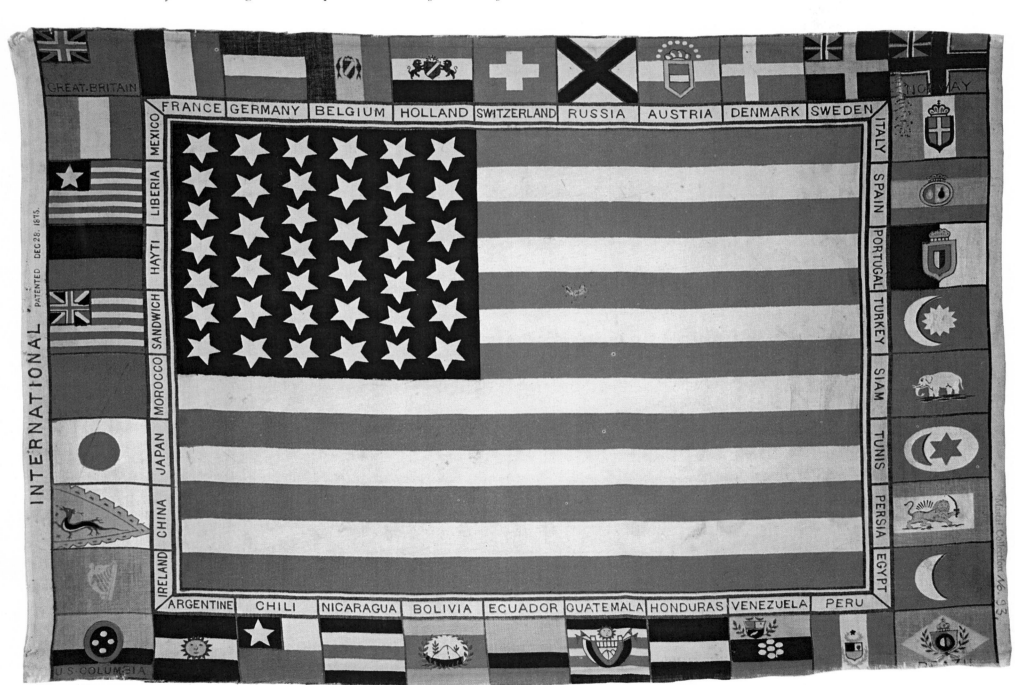

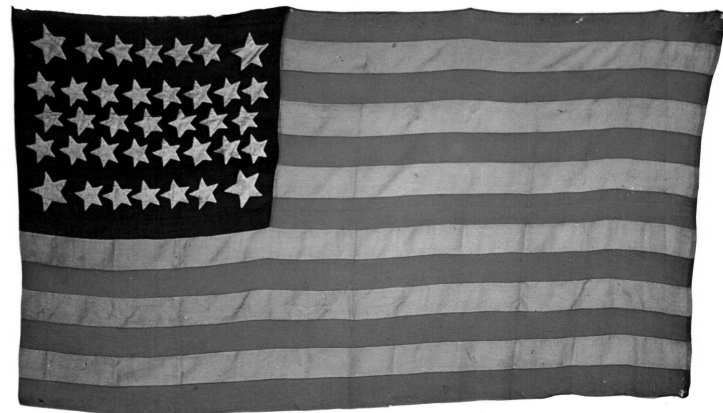

In the canton of the Centennial flag, top, four vertical "rows" of four stars each are firmly wedged inside a "square frame," their rays and the rays of the stars above and below them pointing in different directions. This flag of thirty-eight stars fairly scintillates. <u>Bottom</u>: in the unique "Four-Cornered Flag," of thirty-nine stars, four stellar performers—one at each corner—appear to lead the top and bottom rows in a measured minuet, while the three "staggered" ranks between act as a corps de ballet.

would be accomplished more easily than that of the earlier portion. Yet how proud the record of the first hundred years! The number of states had very nearly tripled, the population grown tenfold (from not quite four million to forty million). Surprisingly, the North had found itself richer and stronger at the conclusion of the Civil War, and despite the South's abasement and desolation, the United States now ranked as a world power of the first order. An awareness of the nation's status is clearly set forth in the "global," or "spherical," pattern of stars, one of the most characteristic among flag designs of the Centennial period (page 161). The "American stars" were indeed wandering over the globe, ranging farther than ever before. Hardly a year passed in the decades before and after the First Centennial without proud report of the Stars and Stripes having been planted on some lofty peak or carried into some remote wilderness.

The "age of exploration" in our history, this period might also be called the "age of legend"—the legend of the flag actively in the making. In the receptive climate of the First Centennial, tales which had little if anything to substantiate them became universally accepted, and persist today. One of these was the unwarranted conclusion that the devices on the American flag came from the Washington family coat-of-arms. As the English playwright Martin Farquhar Tupper, most responsible for the idea's popularization, had put it in his verse drama *Washington* (1876): "*...the leader's old crusading blazon...multiplied and magnified...in every way to this,/ Our glorious national banner*"—words assigned to, of all people, Benjamin Franklin. A further note of historical romance was contributed to the era by Sarah Smith Stafford, a respectable maiden lady and daughter of a bonafide Revolutionary veteran, James Bayard Stafford. The lady informed the all-too-gullible American public that the flag of the *Bonhomme Richard* had not gone down, as was believed, with that great ship "sunk in victory." It had in fact been salvaged by her seaman father, to whom it was later presented along with a sword of honor and (unaccountably) a musket. Later accepted by President William McKinley as a gift to the nation, the flag entered the sacred halls of the Smithsonian Institution in Washington, D.C., where it remained enshrined for about two decades before it was established as spurious. The Betsy Ross legend, first brought to light in 1870 by a grandson, bids fair to endure, since it rests entirely on family tradition and can neither be proven nor disproven. The story is too familiar to need repetition. What is often overlooked, however, is that the crucial point is not so much the claim that the flag was made by Betsy Ross as that its *design* was suggested by Washington, and that he did this fully a year before the Flag Resolution. That part of the story has been rejected by all American historians.

But man does not live by fact alone. The tinsel tale may have led to the mining of much true gold, and inspired many a patriotic needlewoman of the Centennial period and since. More important, the emphasis placed in the legend on the "wreath" motif of the so-called "Betsy Ross Flag" may have led indirectly to the creation of the "Great Double-Wreath Flag" of the Centennial (page 118). In its canton, a ring of thirteen stars for the original states is surrounded by an outer circle of twenty-four representing the states admitted afterward until 1876. In a symbolic sense, therefore, Betsy Ross's magic needle also set its mark on what may be the supreme achievement in American flag design in the era just before the onslaught of mechanization.

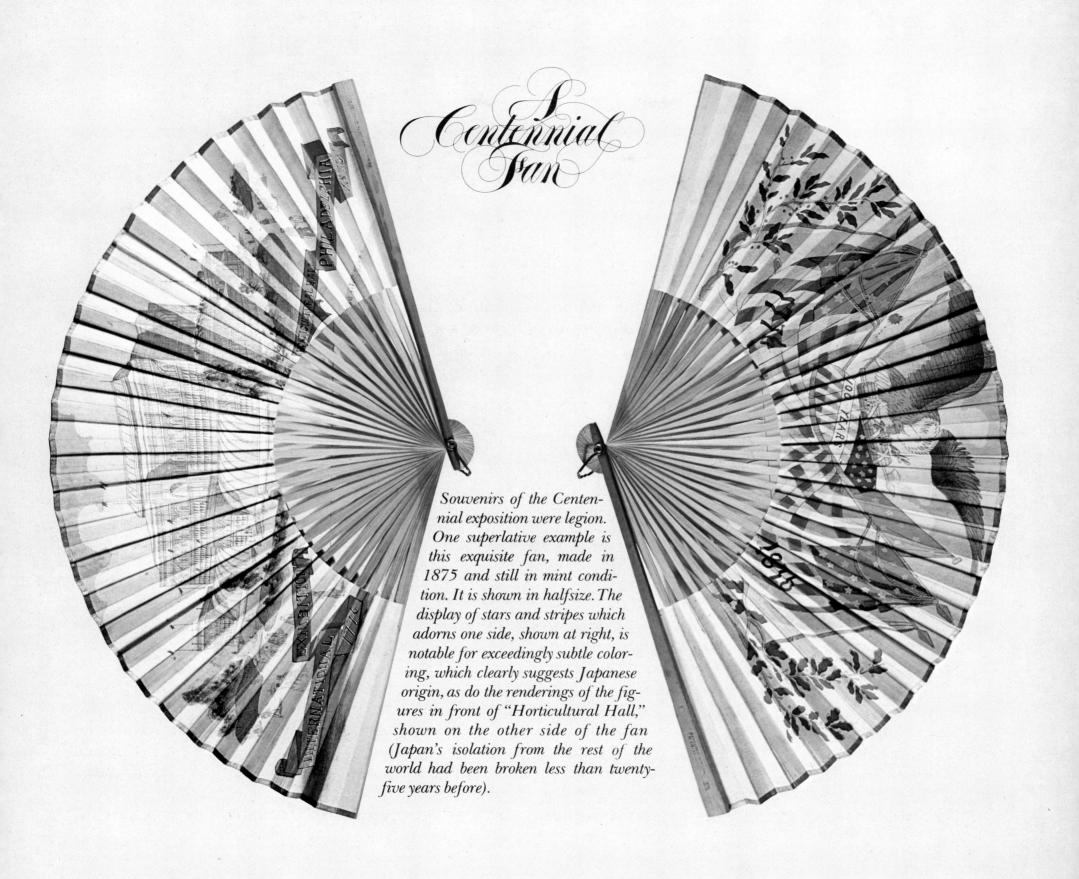

A Centennial Fan

Souvenirs of the Centennial exposition were legion. One superlative example is this exquisite fan, made in 1875 and still in mint condition. It is shown in halfsize. The display of stars and stripes which adorns one side, shown at right, is notable for exceedingly subtle coloring, which clearly suggests Japanese origin, as do the renderings of the figures in front of "Horticultural Hall," shown on the other side of the fan (Japan's isolation from the rest of the world had been broken less than twenty-five years before).

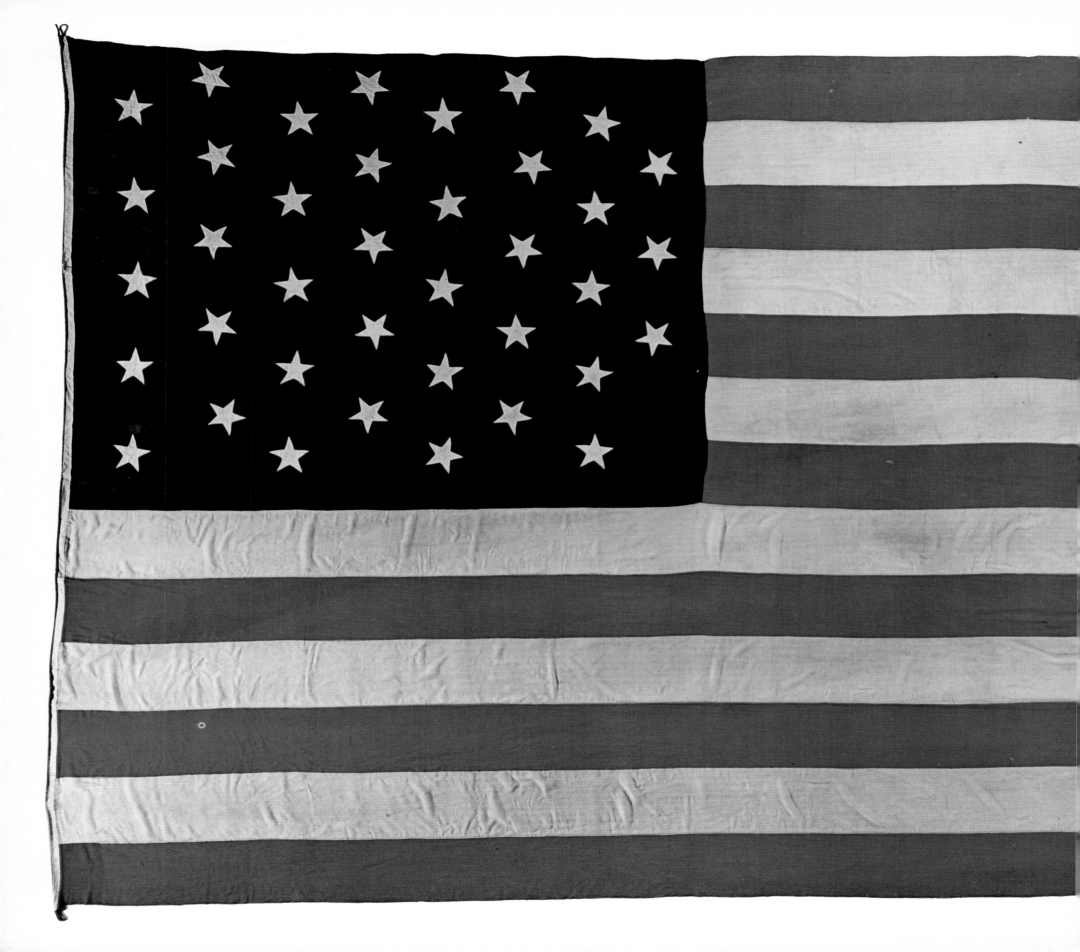

Cometlike, the constellation of thirty-eight stars on this regally elegant giant Centennial flag tapers at one end, space having been allowed at top and bottom of the last vertical "row" for two additional stars to join the fold. But the foresight of the flagmaker was wasted: an official increase in the number of stars did not come about until fourteen years later, when the forty-three-star flag became valid in 1890 following the rapid admission to statehood of North and South Dakota, Montana, Washington, and Idaho.

This thirty-eight-star flag, with space allowed at the right of its canton for two additional stars, is another example of how flagmakers found ways to be economy-minded—a permanent flag representing even then a sizeable investment. <u>Opposite page, right:</u> designed to be displayed upright, as a banner, this commemorative Stars and Stripes bears on its field an inscription and an illustrative vignette with a portrait of Washington. Its canton, on the flag's own left side, would be a serious infraction of present-day flag etiquette.

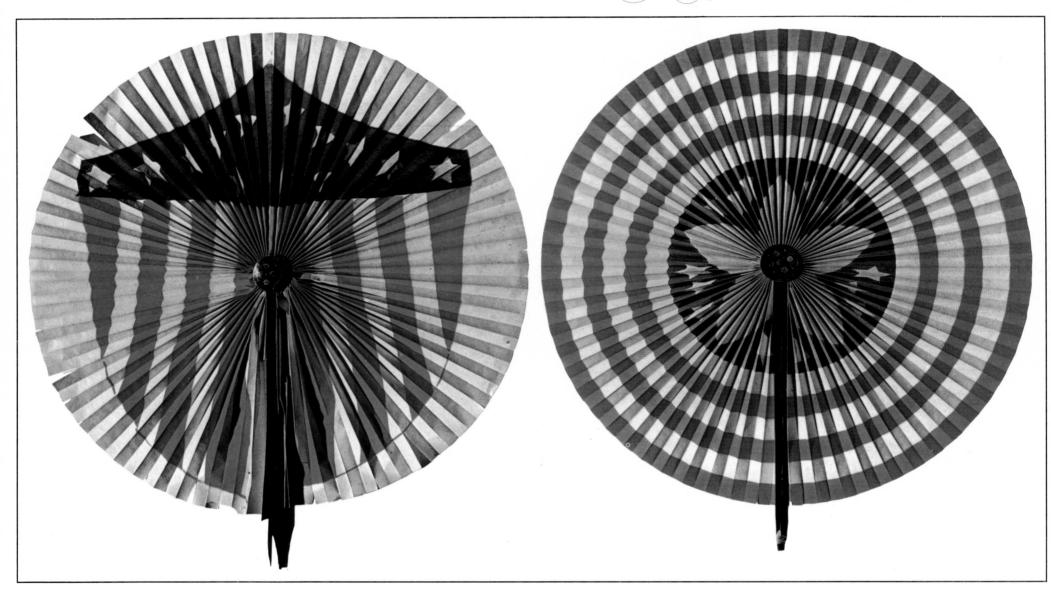

Circular folding fans like these, displaying purely decorative combinations of the devices of the stars and the stripes in the national colors, served to brighten the Centennial celebrations while contributing to the summer comfort of the participants.

No less than twenty Stars and Stripes, with the unofficial count of thirty-nine stars ordered in unequal vertical "rows" of smaller and larger stars (as in the "International Flag," page 162), were brought together to form this superb patriotic quilted coverlet. The reverse was made of repetitions of the patented "Flag of All Nations," whose design combined small flags of many countries, including the United States.

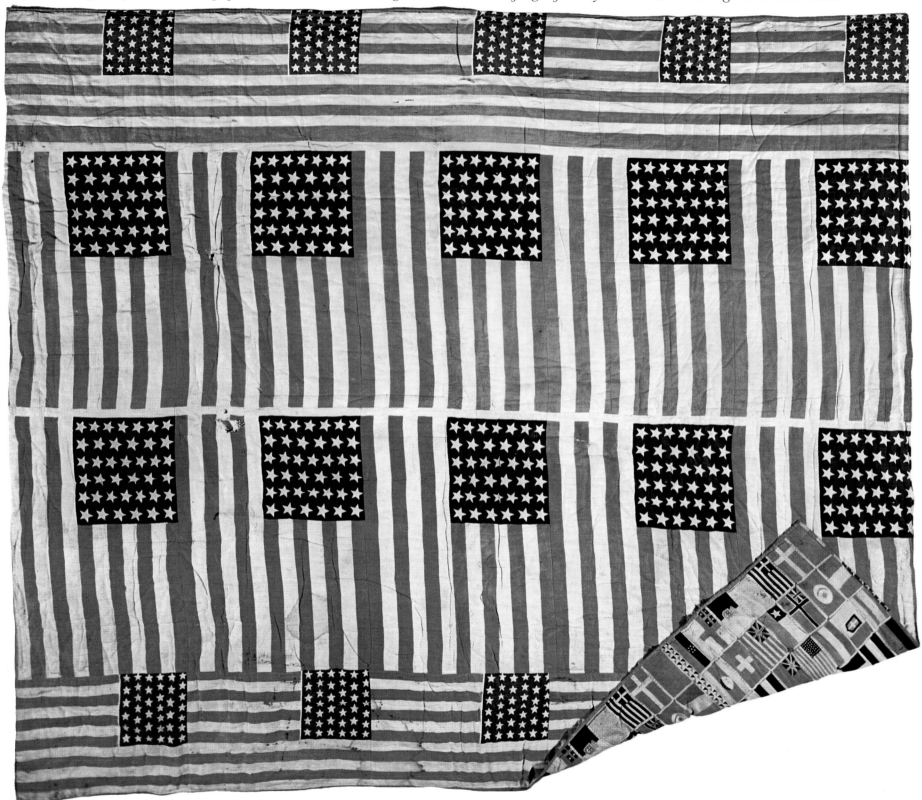

A Swarm of Stars

An array of geometric abstractions—the cantons from various flags of the Centennial period: (1) the elegantly tapered stars of a thirty-eight-star flag of glazed muslin; (2) a close-knit formation particularly notable for the wide, even margin that surrounds, and admirably sets off, the rectangular near-"phalanx" of thirty-eight stars; (3) in contrast to the stars of the previous canton, here they touch the top and bottom of the canton's edge; (4) a twenty-nine-star "double-wreath," with larger corner and center stars—for Iowa; (5) a similar pattern—of thirty-one stars, for California—has an "inlined," or framed, central star, a device in vogue in the 1870's; (6) a union of thirteen stars in which the intersecting crosses of St. George and St. Andrew form a ring of eight stars; (7) the canton of the remarkable "Hour-Glass Flag" (shown in full on page 116); (8) thirty-three stars set (two stars at the canton's left corners) in "global" formation—for Oregon; (9) thirty-eight stars, the two top and two bottom rows of which are "staggered," the two middle rows aligned; (10) another "global" pattern of thirty-eight stars (two stars set at the right corners); (11) thirty-eight stars in "staggered" rows of eight and seven; (12) thirty-nine stars in a diagonal pattern, as used in the "First Flag" of thirteen stars and in the current flag of fifty stars.

6

7

8

9

10

11

12

The Flag in Daily Life

The great clock dial shown opposite is appropriately symbolic: throughout the nation's history, the Stars and Stripes in one guise or another has accompanied and inspired Americans during every waking hour—and, one assumes, given patriotic dye to their dreams too. The singlemindedness of the flag cult has been perhaps a unique phenomenon. Not that all peoples at all times have not cherished their national emblems and taken pleasure, as well, in displaying them on objects of daily use. But Americans, by the very youth of their nation, are closer to the fount of patriotism—and the flag is, as defined, "our one sole emblem of fidelity." This helps explain the enthusiasm that led Americans, from the start, to depict the beloved symbol in every phase or artifact of daily life. It may also account for the puritanical reaction, in the 1920's and later, that put a halt to such practices. The intention was primarily to stem excesses, but the "backlash" stifled much that was not merely harmless but thoroughly delightful.

A stained-glass clock dial from the 1870's, the numerals cameo-carved.

The detail, top left, of an 1862 textile is from a neckerchief shown in full at bottom right. This Civil War pattern was until recently known only from a baby's christening dress in the Metropolitan Museum of Art, New York—but lacked one element: the pyramid of cannonballs that so aptly punctuates it here. <u>Bottom left:</u> two needlebooks, with petit-point covers depicting the Stars and Stripes of their respective periods (at left, the Civil War, with thirty-six stars; at right, 1836, with twenty-five in the archaic narrow canton). <u>Top right:</u> a Civil War sunshade.

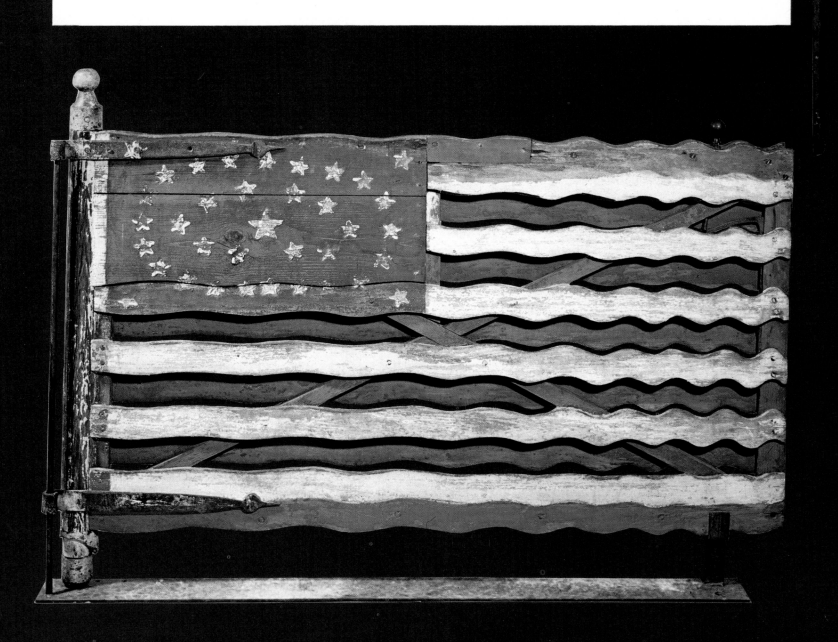

This carved and polychromed "flag pasture-gate" (<u>bottom</u>) from Jefferson County, New York, derives special interest from the adaptation of the flag to a unique function. It is something of a puzzle that the beautiful canton of thirty-eight stars—valid from 1877 to 1890—rests on the "war stripe" although the nation was at peace during the period. <u>Top right</u>: the "Rippled Flag," also of carved and painted wood, has stripes beveled precisely like those on the pasture-gate, in a style that recalls the famous "linen folds" of medieval sculptures. Indeed, "American Gothic" spontaneously comes to mind to define the naïve yet subtle beauty of these two anonymous masterworks of American woodcarving.

In this "Early American History" coverlet (*left*) of the late nineteenth century, each panel depicts, in embroidery stitch, a famous episode of our nation's history, beginning with a Viking expedition and concluding (bottom right corner) with a panel entitled "The First Flag" —which shows the so-called "Betsy Ross," or "wreath," pattern of thirteen stars. *Top right*: detail of one of the flag's stars, appliquéd with buttonhole stitch.

A "friendship" quilt (*opposite page*), at its center the new (1912) flag of forty-eight stars, is painted on velvet and surrounded with multi-colored felt panels embroidered with various designs and signatures. It is an exceedingly bold and colorful example of the genre, expressive of the mood of the last carefree years before the First World War.

Metal artifacts featuring the Stars and Stripes: (1) a bronze Ku Klux Klan belt buckle (late nineteenth century); (2) a Japanese silver box, at upper left, with enameled American and Japanese flags on its cover (with Oriental courtesy, the Stars and Stripes is given place of honor on the right) and, at bottom right, a German brass pill box with Imperial eagle and German and American flags enameled on the hinged cover—both c. 1912; (3) a steel chocolate mold; (4) a silver matchbox of the Civil War period; (5) a "flag cane," for use on patriotic or political occasions (when not in such use, the miniature Stars and Stripes of thirty-nine stars was rolled around the stick, which was then pushed inside the japanned tube that served as a cane).

This patriotic "wheelman" proudly astride his "high-rider" (c. 1890–1895) obviously felt no qualms about the decorations on his vehicle. Actual flags radiated from the hubs of the wheels, forming "Great Stars" (or "Great Flowers") while the cycle was at rest; in motion, the effect was kaleidoscopic.

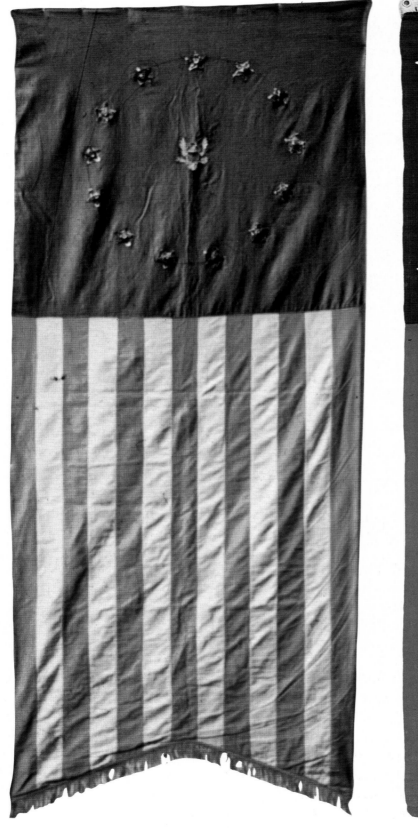

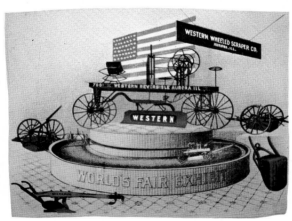

An elegant, fringed ceremonial banner (<u>opposite page, left</u>) shows the symbolic thirteen stars of the "Third Maryland" pattern; the banner dates from c. 1890. <u>Opposite page, right:</u> a thirteen-star "boat flag," its headband bearing the stenciled inscription "U.S. Ensign No. 7—Navy Yard, N.Y.—April 1891." From the start, the Navy enjoyed the privilege of placing on its small boat flags only thirteen stars rather than the full complement; the custom was discontinued by executive order of President Woodrow Wilson in 1916. <u>Top:</u> an "advertising flag" of the Centennial period. This "flaglet" is a purely imaginary version of the first Stars and Stripes; it was meant primarily to inspire patriotism in children and was therefore a civic contribution of the merchant involved. <u>Bottom:</u> some display of patriotism was almost mandatory in business cards of the late nineteenth century. The two at left and center, undeniably "surrealist," are arresting. Less inspired perhaps, but as startling, the card at right (Louisville, 1878) pairs the Stars and Stripes with a giant "Magnolia Ham" under the benevolent eye of canny shopper Uncle Sam.

SONGS OF THE FLAG

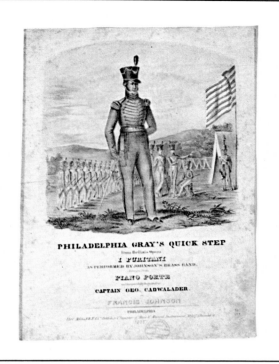

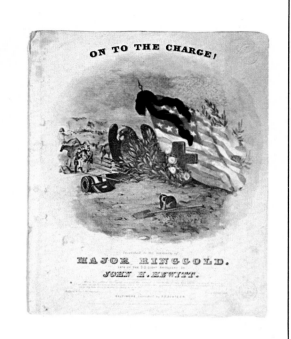

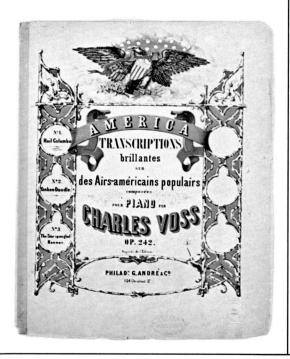

Patriotic song sheets furnish valuable insights on popular concepts of both the use and design of the flag. During the period 1835–1876 (pages 184 and 185) the connotation of the flag is martial and there is repeated use of multi-colored "American stripes" as well as heraldic stars. The "Song of a Thousand Years" (1863) peers, however, into the future (<u>bottom center</u>): in its flag, no less than forty-six stars stud the canton.

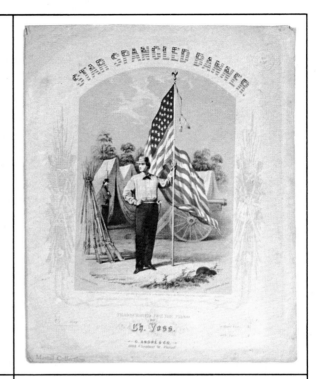
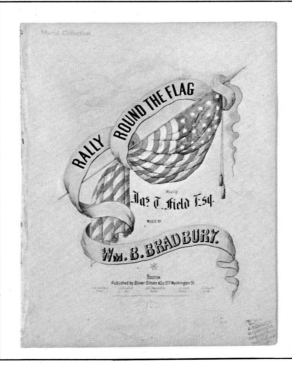
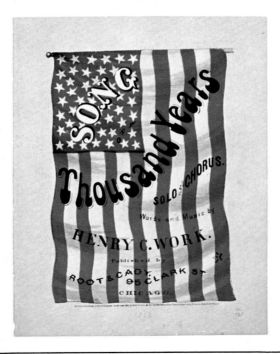

SONGS OF THE FLAG

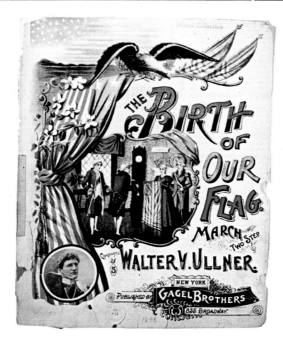

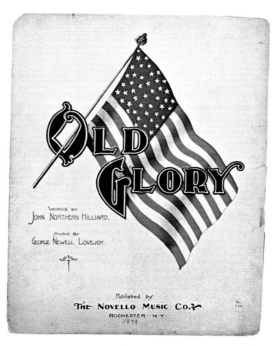

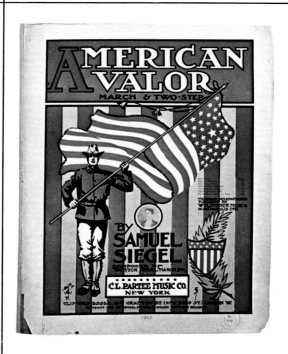

Examples dating from the period 1887–1919 (pages 186 and 187) include not only the usual military concept of the flag (inspired by the Spanish-American and First World wars) but subjects of patriotic and civic interest: the Betsy Ross legend, in "The Birth of Our Flag" (1898); pride in national wealth and power, in "Under Freedom's Banner" (1905); an awareness of ethnic conflict, in "I'm an American, That's All" (1915); and a toast to victory, in a 1919 combination music sheet/calendar.

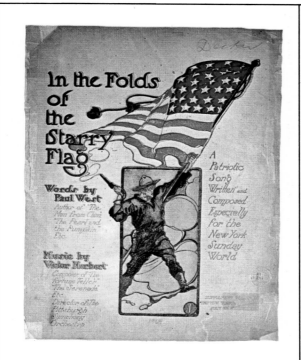

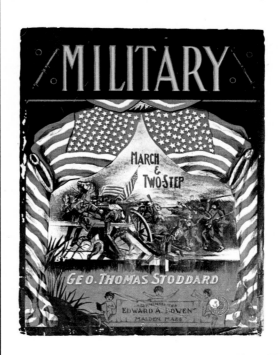

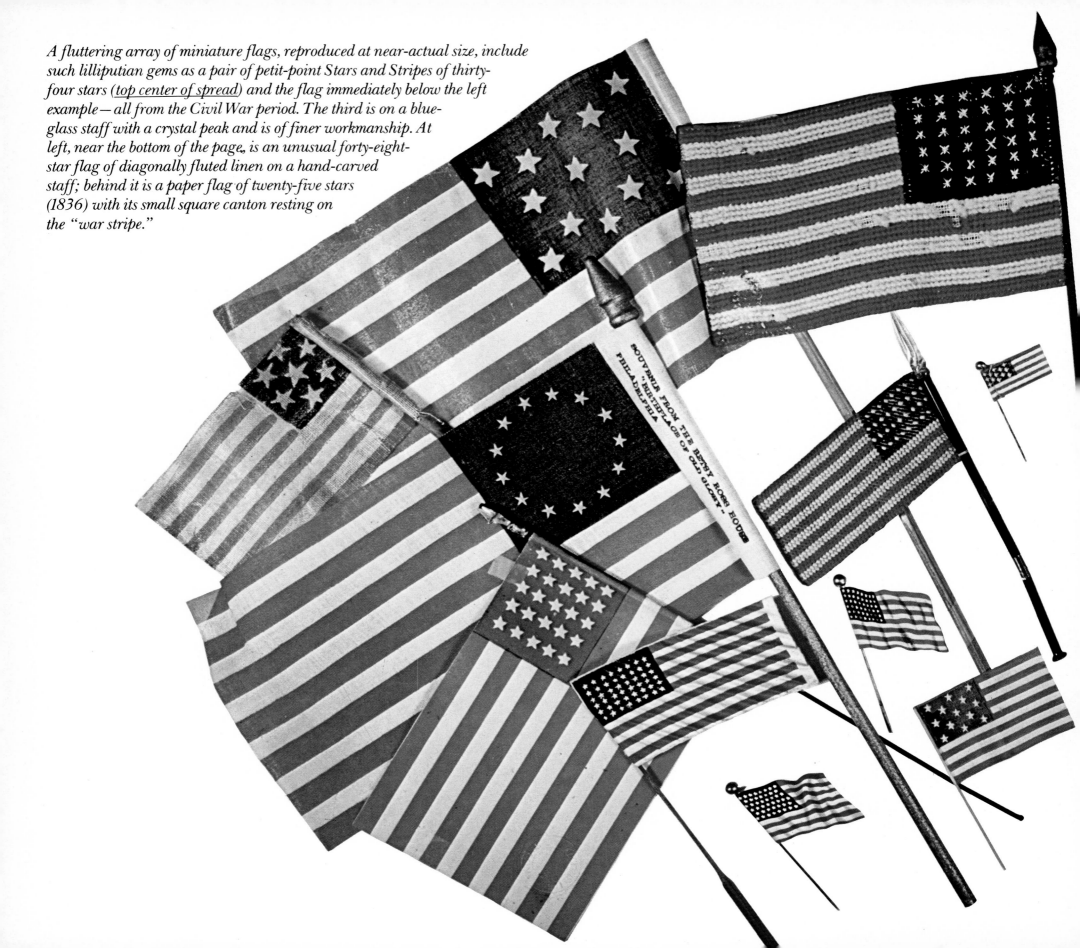

A fluttering array of miniature flags, reproduced at near-actual size, include such lilliputian gems as a pair of petit-point Stars and Stripes of thirty-four stars (<u>top center of spread</u>) and the flag immediately below the left example—all from the Civil War period. The third is on a blue-glass staff with a crystal peak and is of finer workmanship. At left, near the bottom of the page, is an unusual forty-eight-star flag of diagonally fluted linen on a hand-carved staff; behind it is a paper flag of twenty-five stars (1836) with its small square canton resting on the "war stripe."

The second flag down from top left is in woven silk and commemorates the centenary of New York Public Schools; below it is a fringed-ribbon flag with woven names of the presidential and vice-presidential candidates of the 1889 campaign. The third flag down from top right, a minute masterpiece of the weaver's art, celebrates the First Centennial; on its reverse, the inscription is worked in red on the white stripes. Immediately below it, a fragile paper flag (1859) still displays (thirty-three) six-pointed heraldic stars and red stripes edged with thread-thin blue lines. _Across bottom of spread:_ "lapel flags" of varying denomination.

The Flag in Daily Life

The Star-Spangled Banner waves proudly astern a forerunner of the Yankee clipper ships (*opposite page, top left*) on a hatbox manufactured, *c.* 1835, for Joseph S. Tillinghast of New Bedford, Massachusetts. *Bottom left*: a double-sided gameboard—for Parcheesi and Checkers—from *c.* 1835. *Top right*: in this wallpaper distributed by John & Charles Cook of Boston, *c.* 1835, the flag theme is particularly emphasized. The sailing ship at upper left flaunts not only an ensign of the "American stripes," shown in red and black (black, in this two-color print, is the equivalent of blue), but also a swallow-tailed pennant with the same colors and a tricolor "long pennant" of red, black, and light yellow (yellow here standing in for white). The steamship at lower right carries only the ensign and long pennant, and is symbolically set within a framework of starry-blossomed boughs. *Bottom right*: a swath of textile, from *c.* 1830. (The maker of the Know-Nothing flag shown on page 26 used the Washington medallion from material of this pattern.)

A variety of patriotic textiles: (1) a square silk flag of thirty-nine-stars as pocket handkerchief (1889), with wide hem and open-work; (2) an Uncle Sam pillow cover, patented in 1904; (3) a commemorative textile (1889) with medallions of Washington and the incumbent President, Benjamin Harrison; (4) a silk souvenir bandanna commemorating OUR ASSASSINATED PRESIDENTS (1901); (5) a silk handkerchief with a canton of stars at each corner (*c.* 1890); (6) an embroidered pillow cover entitled OLD GLORY (*c.* 1890).

1

4

2

5

3

6

Envelopes with printed semblances of the Stars and Stripes occupying the entire address side had already been popular during the Civil War. Later, one ingenious and patriotic correspondent went one better, using an actual miniature flag to cover his envelope (fully opened, left center) and then sealing the folds with red wax, stamping, and sending it on "c/o of Uncle Sam." Its postmark: July 4, 1893. Bottom left: a forty-four-star printed flag envelope postmarked October 15, 1902.

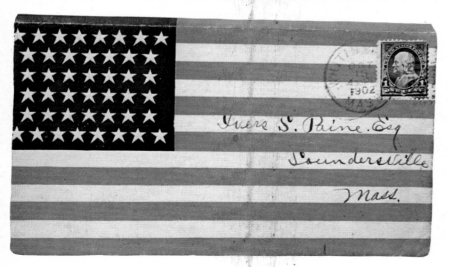

A flag is the cover of a blotter pad, top right; it is handpainted, but though the canton holds the forty-five stars of 1896 its stripes are the nine often used in the Revolutionary period. Right center: at left, an advertising postcard with a portrait of Washington in the canton and an inscription on the "flag's" white stripes; at right, a souvenir postcard of the Pan-American Exposition in Buffalo, 1901, with a buffalo head in a circular medallion in the canton (the card is unused, but it might well have carried home the news of the assassination of President McKinley at the opening ceremonies).

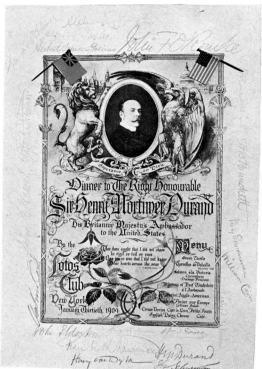

The hand-painted flag of forty-four stars at left was used at the Lotos Club, New York—together with a pendant piece representing the Union Jack—for festivities in honor of "the Right Honourable Sir Henry Mortimer Durand, His Britannic Majesty's Ambassador to the United States" on January 30, 1904. (The flag was one star behind the times.) <u>Top center:</u> a cover of the souvenir menu bears numerous autographs, including that of the guest of honor. Small paper flags are pinned to the cover.

A handsome "medal" of "The Independent Order of Odd Fellows" (<u>top right</u>) bears two extraneous small Stars and Stripes of fluted silk on its white satin band. The symbol of the "All-Seeing Eye" recalls the Masonic associations in the American flag's early history.

In 1912, a Chinese artisan made a new "flower flag" of forty-eight stars bloom on the brooch of champleve enamel and silver filigree at top left. The stars, globular, look like berries or tight round buds. *Top center:* on a Centennial silk bandanna, the American flag, inside a "wreath" of stars, has thirty-six stars unusually set in an oval "double-wreath" enclosing two central stars. *Bottom:* this slate plaque from a Grand Army of the Republic headquarters memorializes the famous association of Civil War veterans and displays a flag with thirty-eight stars (Centennial period) in an outsized canton. The "marble" border, painted in *trompe-l'oeil*, is actually a part of the slate slab.

G.A.R.

Further decorative uses of the flag: (1) a "flag fan" of Oriental workmanship (1912); (2) an apron, the pattern of the material, with flag motif, commemorating the hundredth anniversary of the cultivation of cotton in the United States (1891); (3) a "Scottish" velvet bonnet, bead-embroidered with a stylized Stars and Stripes, by Mohawk Indians, c. 1900; (4) the "figurehead" to some rampant tin lizzie, this truly "kinetic" radiator cap with revolving, wind-activated flanges was patented on September 4, 1917.

THE LADY OF THE FLAG

There is no doubt that a female "spirit" has ever presided over the destinies of this nation. Known in turn by many names—the "Goddess (or Spirit) of Liberty," "America," and "Liberty," in the nation's earliest days—she became known as "Columbia" as her empire spread across the continent, and was deified as "the Union" during the Civil War. *Right:* a neo-classical figure of "America" (1801), with Niagara in the background, holding a Revolutionary pike and cap and a composite flag displaying an eagle on the "American stripes" and a rattlesnake on a blue canton. *Bottom center:* a music sheet of 1855 showing an actress in George Sand attire personifying "Young America." *Bottom left:* by 1861, the solemn war mood is reflected by this music sheet's portrayal of a national "guardian angel."

THE STAR SPANGLED BANNER.

O! long may it wave,
O'er the land of the free,
And the home of the brave.

"Liberty" (<u>left</u>) keeps watch at the tomb of "the Father of His Country" in this American chenille embroidery, with painting, done in 1800. <u>Top center:</u> Currier & Ives portrayed the American tutelary figure in crinoline and starry diadem. <u>Bottom center:</u> a delicate personification of the young Republic against a billowing flag of twenty-six stars (1837). <u>Bottom right:</u> "the Union" tramples on the shackles of slavery.

Let this be our motto — In God is our trust
And the star-spangled Banner, in Glory shall wave
O'er the Land of the Free, and the Home of the Brave.

AMERICA

Flags of the Nations' Series

Gradually, in the last decades of the nineteenth century, the matronly majesty of "Columbia" made way for a second, more graceful and sprightly figure: her daughter? "Miss America" or "Miss Liberty," as the charmer came to be known the world over. On pages 198 and 199, she models her changing wardrobe—from the subtle elegances of the mauve decade and its wreaths of American Beauty roses, to the immaculate,

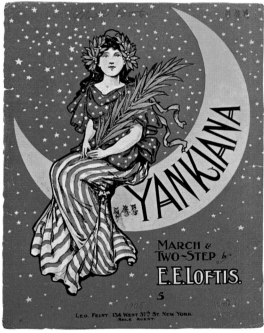

cool look of the "All-American Girl," and culminating in the transcendental chic of a sublimated flapper with a galaxy of stars and cataract of stripes (by Louis Icard, 1927).

No evidence is found until the mid-nineteenth century of a special relationship between children and the American flag. One cannot imagine a group of boys and girls waving small flags to greet President Washington—as they are seen doing, in the drawing opposite, for Major General George McClellan in Frederick, Maryland, on September 12, 1862. (Note a detail in the foreground: the flag wound as a sash around the girl's waist.) Yet surely patriotism in earlier days was no less; children were simply not encouraged to infringe upon adult preoccupations. During the trying days of the Civil War, however, patriotic sentiment—in South as well as North—came to be expressed so constantly and with such undisguised emotion that it could in some measure be understood and shared by little ones. Mothers taught their daughters to make "flaglets" for the children's own use or as prized gifts. _Top right:_ little golden stars, thirteen in number, decorate the canton of this Civil War "flaglet"; in a pair of small flags of the same period (_opposite page_), the stripes are of silk ribbon and the sparkle of the stars (on navy-blue cantons) is suggested by use of round silver sequins. _Bottom left:_ a Civil War daguerreotype shows a solemn little "zouave" holding a flag that appears to have had a light-blue canton of unusual pattern. _Bottom center:_ a beguiling print, "Our Colors," by the Connecticut publishers E. B. & E. C. Kellogg. _Bottom right:_ the "Pic Nic of the Fourth of July—A Day to Be Remembered" (1864), by Lilly Martin Spencer (1822–1902), one of America's foremost woman artists of the nineteenth century. Symbolically and artistically, the baby waving the flag is the composition's apex.

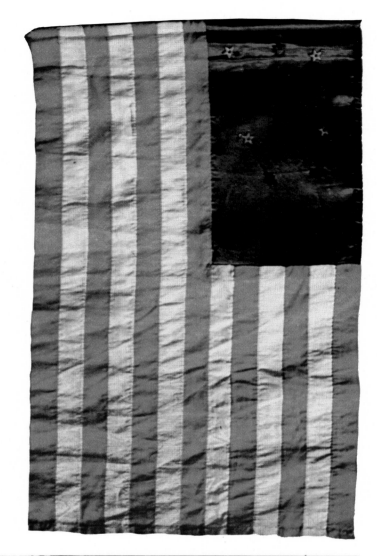

OUR COLORS.

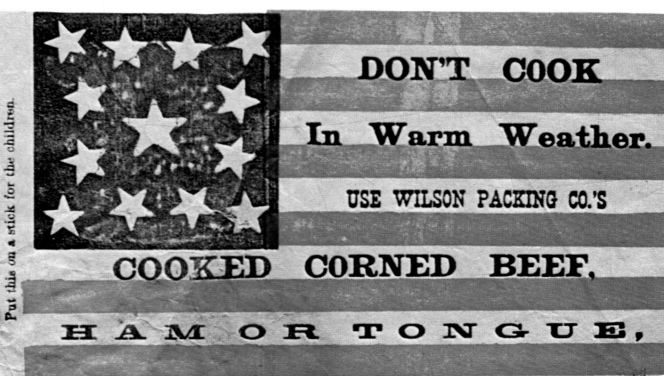

Put this on a stick for the children.

DON'T COOK
In Warm Weather.
USE WILSON PACKING CO.'S
COOKED CORNED BEEF,
HAM OR TONGUE,
IN 2, 4 OR 6 POUND CANS.

The mood of the post-Centennial decades was hearty and exuberant. The bright and lively illustrations for juvenile books of the period expressed it well. <u>Bottom left and center</u>: "Yankee Doodle/Uncle Sam" strides the world, "upon his little pony"; and a mighty future defender of the flag prepares for his task.

The mass production of small printed-muslin, as well as paper, flags made them widely available. Mothers frequently bought them for their children. <u>Top left</u>: this Centennial example, in printed muslin, is one of a set of five that bore, each, the name of one of five sisters; it belonged to the youngest, Edith Scott, whose name appears twice— once in her baby scrawl and again in a maturer hand. <u>Top right</u>: a very rare, because exceedingly fragile, small silk-paper flag retains the original instructions for use on the wide margin at its hoist side.

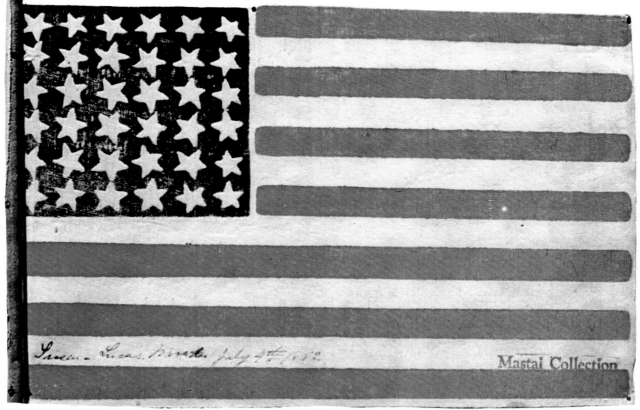

A toy drum (<u>left</u>) carries flags and a portrait of Admiral George Dewey. <u>Top left, center, and right</u>: an illustration from a book on the flag for children, by Francis Scott Key III; a stand-up business card with a little "Betsy Ross" of the sewing-machine age; a chromolithograph on which a child-symbol of the nation's future triumphs over tragedies of the past. <u>Bottom right</u>: one of a set of two children's flags bearing the names, respectively, of two sisters, and the date July 4, 1872. (The thirty-six-star canton was behind the times.)

THE FLAG IN POLITICS

Political demonstrations in the United States have always been distinguished, from their equivalents in European lands, by what might easily seem redundant display of the national flag. The justification for this is that, from the start, the Stars and Stripes has been not merely the national emblem but, as well, "the flag of the free," the guardian of American liberties. Patriotic and civic pride are, in fact, combined in the illustration at top left: a music sheet of 1840 depicting the elegant cavalcade of the Whig Convention at the foot of the Bunker Hill Monument, unfinished but nevertheless topped with the flag for the event. _Right_: a Currier & Ives political print showing the stern countenance of General Winfield Scott, hero of the Mexican War, with that of his co-candidate, courted national suffrage in 1852 (unsuccessfully). _Opposite page_: a great flag of thirty-four stars bears an admirable—but still unidentified—motto to end all political mottoes. (Standing beside it, author Boleslaw Mastai.)

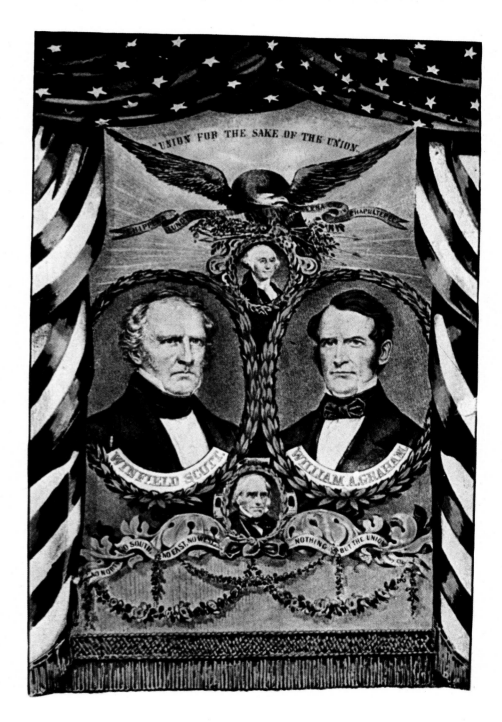

THE FLAG IN POLITICS

General McClellan, idol of the Army in the early days of the Civil War, stood in 1864 as presidential candidate against Lincoln. He was defeated by an overwhelming majority of the soldier vote, who had learned by then to prefer "Father Abraham" to "the American Napoleon." McClellan's personal flags during this campaign were, on staffs of precious wood with silver peaks and halyards, the two silk standards shown on pages 206 and 207 both in full and in detail. Designed to stand at right and left of the speaker, they bear inscriptions on one side only. The details show the workmanship of embroidery: two-toned silk floss was used for the lettering and the golden stars were built up in the crystal pattern of five conjoined lozenges, refinements that could only be appreciated at close quarters. Whereas the motto is still in pristine condition on one flag, McClellan's name was later pricked out on the other, probably to allow use of the flag at large—and it does evidence far more wear and tear than its twin. <u>Bottom left:</u> an 1861 music sheet dedicated to McClellan.

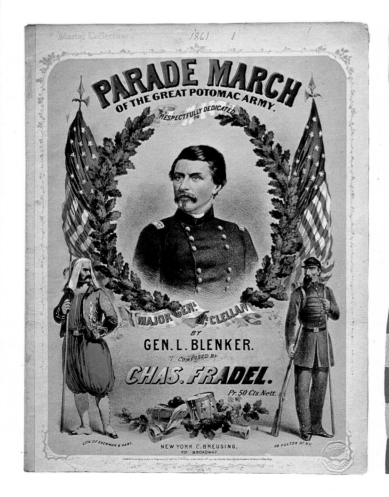

THE FLAG IN POLITICS

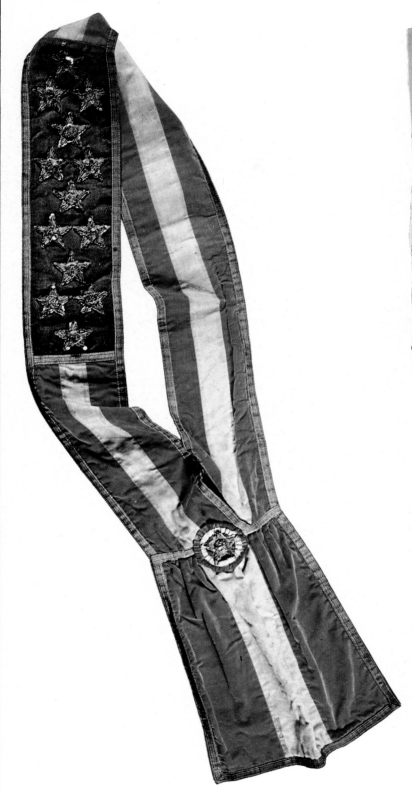

During the presidential campaign of 1868, General Ulysses S. Grant, Republican candidate, protested indignantly the use of his portrait on the canton of flags. In 1884, candidates James G. Blaine and John A. Logan—or at least their campaign manager—did not share such scruples: their portraits did appear, set amid the thirty-eight stars then valid, on very handsome silk printed flags (*top right*). Far less objectionable, by comparison, was the inclusion of their names on a flag with a starry canton that echoes the "American stripes" and does not duplicate the national flag (*opposite page, left*).

A baldric (*left*) of the type sported by some presidential candidates suggests a Stars and Stripes draped as a sash, with part of the canton on the shoulder of the wearer. It is in fact only a flat, narrow band made of extremely fine silk velvet, with silver stars and border. *Opposite page, right:* a flag of thirty-six stars set in the characteristic Centennial "spherical" pattern (one star at each corner) was made to serve for the presidential campaign of 1889—a band was added to the outer edge bearing the name of candidate Benjamin Harrison (the letterer reversed the "S"). The flag's canton hides a "Great Star" camouflaged in the manner of that shown on page 110.

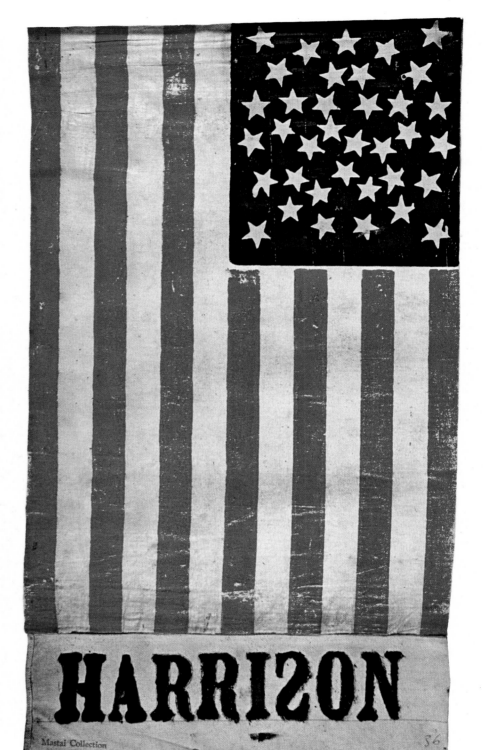

PROTECTION & PROSPERITY

OUR CHOICE
HARRISON
AND
MORTON

HARRI2ON

Mastai Collection

THE FLAG IN POLITICS

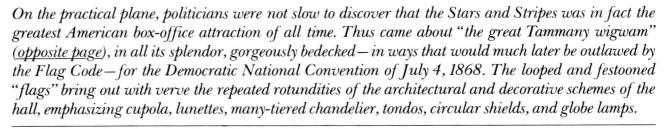

On the practical plane, politicians were not slow to discover that the Stars and Stripes was in fact the greatest American box-office attraction of all time. Thus came about "the great Tammany wigwam" (_opposite page_), in all its splendor, gorgeously bedecked—in ways that would much later be outlawed by the Flag Code—for the Democratic National Convention of July 4, 1868. The looped and festooned "flags" bring out with verve the repeated rotundities of the architectural and decorative schemes of the hall, emphasizing cupola, lunettes, many-tiered chandelier, tondos, circular shields, and globe lamps.

Candidates McKinley and Garret A. Hobart, in 1896, appear in a surprisingly discreet political token: a "flag brooch" (_top left and center_) which opens, book-wise, to reveal their portraits within rather than upon the national symbol.

Political ribbons (_bottom_) of various dates. A beautiful dark-red and silver Garfield band (1880) has the candidate's name and motto on the flag's stripes. The pert New York State League ribbon loops an actual miniature Stars and Stripes bow-tie fashion at its top.

The imposing banner on the opposite page was made to bear a band with the wishful motto of Horatio Seymour, Democratic candidate against General Grant in 1868. The addition is dwarfed, however, both by the size of the flag (24 feet long by 19 feet wide) and by the undoubted splendor of its design, kindred to the "medallion" flags on pages 118 to 121. The design of this great "double-wreath" of thirty-six stars and one central star (valid 1867–1877) was selected for duplication by the New York Metropolitan Museum of Art on the museum's hundredth anniversary in 1970.

A William Jennings Bryan political poster (bottom left) incorporates the flag, as does a Republican pamphlet cover bearing likenesses of President Lincoln and General Grant (bottom right).

The Triumphant Banner

Between 1890 and 1908, all but two of the last Western territories became states, the number of stars on the American flag increasing from forty-three to forty-six. The additions made little difference, however, in the designs of the cantons of the four flags in use during the period: each displayed its stars in a pattern of parallel rows—which fulfilled their purpose adequately but can scarcely be called inspired. Although such monotonous simplicity seems a puzzling choice for an age whose tastes frankly ran to opulence and over-ornateness, one surmises that the reason little creativity was wasted on the cantons of the four flags may have been their temporary nature. Many Americans were genuinely convinced that future increase in the number of stars would not stop at the inclusion of the two Southwestern territories—New Mexico and Arizona—almost any day or, more remotely, the frozen wilderness of Alaska, but would extend to our newly acquired Pacific and Caribbean possessions. On June 14, 1901—Flag Day—one patriotic orator declared without hesitation that "political astronomers…must

Patriotic belle of the turn of the century (an oilcolor print).

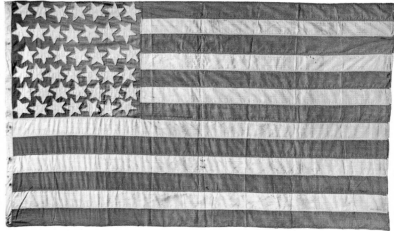

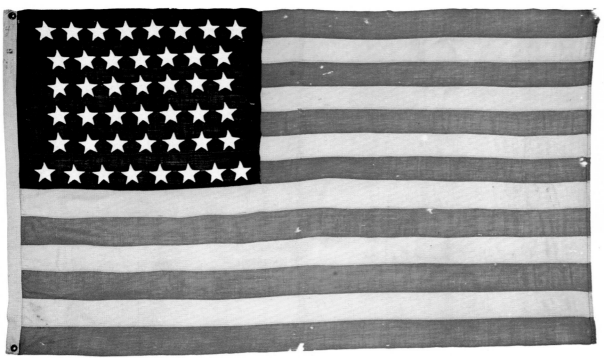

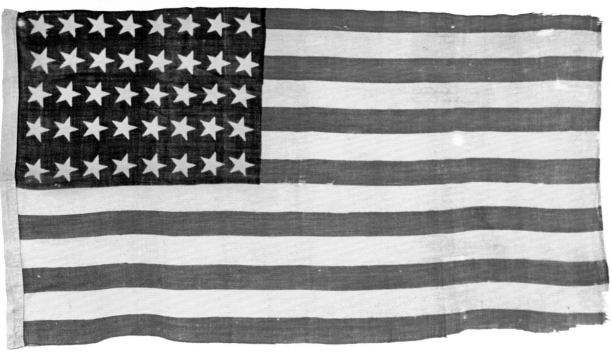

In November 1889, four territories were raised to statehood in such swift succession that they might almost be considered "quadruplets." North and South Dakota came in as "twins" on November 2, Montana was "born" on November 8, and Washington followed on November 11. The four new stars were not to be added to the thirty-eight-star constellation until July 4, 1890, but exactly one day before that event a fifth star joined them—for Idaho. But, while the forty-three-star flag had official existence for one year, for all practical purposes it was "stillborn": the state of Wyoming was admitted on July 10, 1890, raising the total states to forty-four. That number of stars in the flag became valid on July 4, 1891. During this confusing period, flags of varying numbers of stars were therefore flown. <u>Top left</u>: a regulation flag of forty-four stars. <u>Bottom left</u>: a printed flag of forty stars that indicates a harried manufacturer's efforts to keep up with the unofficial increase. <u>Top right and canton opposite page</u>: a home production of forty-two stars, partly machine-sewn, has a happy, jostling crowd of stars aligned haphazardly on a canton now bleached in part. The canton's tint is now pleasingly graded from deep ultramarine to dawn blue, but can never originally have been any darker than lapis-lazuli.

The Spanish-American War was fought under the flag of forty-five stars, which became official on July 4, 1896. _Opposite page:_ an example that is both unusually handsome and of historical significance. The distant stars on a night-blue canton herald a new era when the preference would be for severe coloring and chastened design; the increasing precision of mechanical production of flags furthered this preference. The inscription on the flag's headband (_detail, bottom opposite page_) bears the signature of an officer, J. R. Thompson, who received the flag following the war, in souvenir of his command. In addition, the band bears the hand-printed words "I. U.S. Vol. Eng. N.Y. ARMY OF INVASION, 2nd Bat. Co. K. PORTO RICO, 1898" and a long list of places where the flag did duty. _Bottom left:_ a square banner honoring Admiral Dewey. _Right:_ a Filipino woven mat with the Stars and Stripes and Philippine national flag conjoined beneath an American eagle.

THE
HERO

ADMIRAL DEWEY

OF
MANILA

In accordance with the policy of President Theodore Roosevelt—"Speak softly but carry a big stick"—an impressive fleet of twenty-eight American warships was sent on a round-the-world cruise of "good will" in 1909. The tour also made evident the scope and readiness of U.S. naval power. For enterprising merchants this meant a rare opportunity to produce a bumper crop of souvenirs (most of them were made in Brooklyn), such as the opalescent-satin pillow covers and sachets shown against an enlarged detail of a sachet depicting the "Atlantic Battleship Fleet." The most interesting feature of these souvenirs is the utilitarian use to which it was still possible to put the flag: miniature Stars and Stripes were made to serve as an inner pocket for each sachet; the receptacle would be reserved solely for the patriotic purpose of preserving all the mementoes sent home to fond mothers and sweethearts by their heroes abroad. On the cover of the red-bordered sachet at center is an old photograph of a battleship. At far right, the same sachet is open, showing the double-frame (above the flag) for personal photographs.

—ATLA

IC·BATTLESHIP·FLEET··

The Fort Keogh Flag

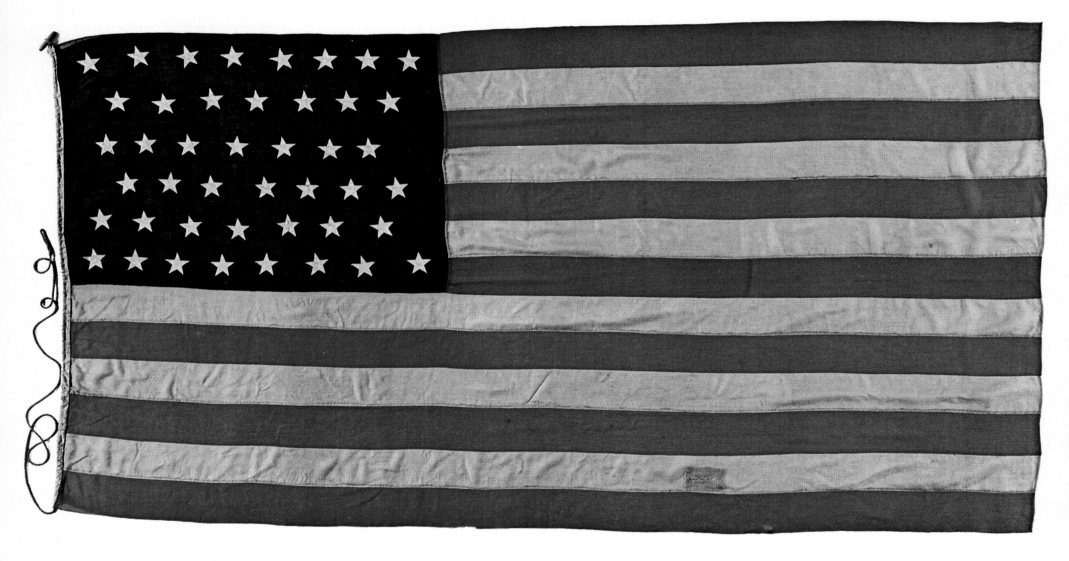

This flag of forty-four stars was floated over Fort Keogh, Montana. The garrison was probably named after Captain Myles W. Keogh, who fell at the battle fought at the junction of the Big Horn and Little Big Horn rivers in South Dakota in late June 1876, where Colonel George Custer and his troop of two hundred men were wiped out by the superior forces of Chief Sitting Bull. Fort Keogh was notable not only as the largest and most important military post on the Northwest frontier but as the scene of government experiments in the training of Indian scouts. There, under the flag shown here, Lieutenant S. C. Robertson and Lieutenant E. W. Casey formed their Crow scouts into the First Irregular Cavalry unit. Frederic Remington spent some time at Fort Keogh, and recorded daily life in and around the fort in numerous sketches.

discover new stars…and then locate them upon the blue field, as will be the case of Cuba and Porto Rico."

Condoned by some as expansionism, condemned by others as imperialism—and, in fact, a revival of the earlier doctrine of Manifest Destiny—the restlessness of the national mood at the century's end is appropriately, if accidentally, seen in the vertical "rows" of stars in the cantons of this period; parallelism is observed only on the horizontal plane. The ranks, therefore, do not appear stable but instead seem to be moving—shifting and advancing toward some undetermined goal (see pages 222 and 225). The effect was, of course, not attributable to flagmakers' personal touch or plan—by this time the manufacture of flags was entirely mechanized. Such slight variations as may still be found in Stars and Stripes of the period generally represent no more than the "handwriting style" of the machines that made them.

But if creativity in American flag design had come to a standstill, the cult of the flag was never more fervent. The Centennial exposition of 1876, in particular, had ushered in what might be termed "the age of exhibitions," or "of anniversaries." Most exemplary of these was the great Columbian fair of 1893 in Chicago, where displays of flags, overwhelming in quantity if not in quality, played a prominent role. No restraint whatever was placed on the decorative use of the national flag, which was therefore draped, looped, and festooned in all possible manner. Had such practices been challenged, precedents could have been cited. In 1824, the hallowed Star-Spangled Banner itself had served to decorate the interior of Washington's war tent, raised once again, at Fort McHenry for the return reception of General Lafayette; given the enormous size of the flag, it appears that it must have had to be draped in some way, and this seems confirmed by the use of the word "adorn" in the contemporary records. In 1833, Savannah had celebrated the second inauguration of President Andrew Jackson "in the most patriotic style," climaxing the day with a splendid ball; over each window of the grand ballroom was a silver star—one for each state—and "the curtain was the flag of the Union." After the Civil War, the War Department's flag museum in Washington, D.C., was similarly decorated, a chronicler noting: "The windows and doors of this room are shaded by flags fastened at the top and looped back at the sides, in the manner of window curtains." Many far more revealing examples could be cited. What matters, of course, is that at no time had disrespect been intended.

Nor, at the close of the nineteenth century, had printing over the American flag yet been outlawed. No qualms were felt about putting inscriptions on the field, or even on the canton, for political or commercial purposes. Furthermore, the development of color printing on a wide scale and at low prices gave impetus to the expression of patriotic sentiments in printed form. This was the age of patriotic postcards, which deluged the nation like the myriad snowflakes of some tricolored blizzard. Sheet music was now mass-produced, and John Philip Sousa's rousing march "The Stars and Stripes Forever" (1897) (page 186) initiated a raft of patriotic melodies that soon were in greater demand following the Spanish-American War. These included such ringing titles, with illustrations to match, as in 1898, "We'll Stand By the Flag" and "We Are Marching to Glory for the Flag." Occasionally, lyrics were created to go along with the tune, such as in "The U.S. Volunteer" (1904), which exulted: *Lead on, Oh Flag so glorious/For You we'll win or die."* In 1907, pop-

When war clouds hover o'er the land we read of heroes brave,
Our officers on land and sea, o'er them we fairly rave;
The real defenders are forgot, the men who fire the gun.
'Tis they who'll shield the Stars and Stripes, God bless them ev'ry mother's son!

He may be wealthy, college bred, perhaps a son of toil,
He volunteers to fight or die, he loves his native soil;
No fame or glory be his, though through him battles are won,
Old Glory will never cease to wave while we have men to fire the gun!

These patriotic souvenir handkerchiefs of sheer moire silk (<u>top left and bottom left</u>) have borders of small American flags. Dating from the Spanish-American War period, their centers portray sentimental military subjects and verses to match. <u>Bottom right:</u> a circular pleated folding fan displays the Stars and Stripes; it has a repeat pattern of the Cuban national flag on both handles. The fan was used during the ceremonies of the termination of United States military protection in Havana on May 20, 1902.

CAMP GREETINGS

By the camp fire they are dreaming of the little home they love
While the quiet stars are beaming like dear watchful eyes above;
A nation's joys are its beautiful boys, with their brave and smiling faces;
In them you'll find the unconquerable mind, that doubt and despair displaces.
O, the boys of Yankee land, you'll find them good and true!
They're ready at command and where there's work to do
He'll never drop and he never will stop, it takes a good lot to do him,
He learns at school the unbreakable rule of never evading duty.

The use of proportionately larger and closer stars on the canton of this forty-five-star flag endows its design with a character totally different from that of the invasion flag on page 218. Its pattern of "staggered" rows is, however, identical to the former's.

ular songwriter E. T. Paull summed up the national exultation in his apt title "The Triumphant Banner."

The patriotic fervor aroused by the Spanish-American conflict inspired the creation of several monster flags rivaling, or even exceeding, the Civil War and Centennial giants. One flag, 120 feet long by 43 feet wide, was raised over the arsenal in Havana on January 1, 1899. The homecoming pennant of Dewey's flagship, the *Olympia,* trailed 500 feet and consequently dipped in the water far in the wake of the vessel. A unique manifestation of the mood of the period was the "living flag." On May 2, 1901, a New Orleans newspaper told how "one thousand colored students of the Southern University greeted President McKinley, en route to San Francisco, by waving bits of red, white and blue bunting so arranged as to make the whole American flag." Other examples of this practice varied only in the number of participants.

Anglo-American amity had been steadily on the rise during the late Victorian period. A British flag was now floated, October 2, 1903, on the Bunker Hill monument in Boston in honor of a visiting British company of artillery. It is significant that, in 1860, when the young Prince of Wales had stood before the monument no British flag was flown. By the turn of the century, it is evident, there was widespread if unofficial hope that "the two branches of the race would perhaps soon be reunited," as one British historian put it. Certainly no objections were raised when Andrew Carnegie raised above his castle of Skibo, in Scotland, what was politely called a "combination flag"—the Stars and Stripes on one side, the Union Jack on the other. It was not the first of its kind. In 1857 and 1858, the U.S. frigate *Niagara,* engaged in laying the Transatlantic Cable, had worn an ensign, designed by promoter Cyrus W. Field himself, which combined "triangular divisions" of the same two national flags; and it was used again on the second expedition, after the Civil War. Whereas not a ripple of protest was heard about the Anglo-American flag, the proposed return of captured Confederate flags to the South (by a War Department order of 1887, approved by President Grover Cleveland) was not received with the same equanimity. Postponed, the return was finally accomplished in 1905 by President Theodore Roosevelt.

In that same year, sad to tell, the would-be Indian state of "Sequoyah" was denied admission to the Union. Two years later, all of that former Indian territory became the forty-sixth state under the name of Oklahoma. But though the nation had spread *"from sea to shining sea,"* no star of her far-flung overseas possessions had yet joined the republican stars of glory of "the triumphant banner." Nevertheless, on April 6, 1909, that banner was indeed destined to hold not a few colonies but the entire world in thrall as the famous dispatch of Arctic explorer Robert E. Peary announced electrifyingly: "Stars and Stripes nailed to the North Pole." In sober fact, the flag was raised on an ice lance. Peary had carried the silken, gold-fringed ensign around his body for several years, planting five successive fragments as markers at the farthest points of his travels. Symbolically, he chose to leave a much larger piece—a band cut across diagonally so as to include both some stars and some stripes—as a permanent record at the apex of the globe. That it was a mere portion was immaterial: in popular imagination, the flag, whole and unblemished, has ever since floated at that frontier of man's adventuring—as far, it was then believed, as man would ever carry the Stars and Stripes.

Flag of the Future

Whether it was a "slip of the machine," or the operator's decision—expressing his belief in our Manifest Destiny—the fact remains that this regulation 1912 American flag (bottom left)—with strong linen band and brass grommets—sports no less than fifty-four stars! Top right: a "dazzler" fan—when the fan is moved up and down, the design appears, optically, to spiral. On the simulated folds, at its heart no less than fifty-one names of states and territories are listed indiscriminately (1900). Center right: a magic-lantern slide showing a Stars and Stripes of forty-two stars—appropriately titled "Flag of the Future" (1889). Bottom right: a remarkably attractive and imaginative poster-diploma of the "Brotherhood of America" displays a pair of large flags crossed: the "First Flag" of thirteen stars and a Stars and Stripes on which a triumphant fifty-eight (the official number was then forty-five) are visible, while a few more are suggested as masked by overlapping elements of the composition (c. 1900).

The Triumphant Banner

A near-centenarian descendant of Betsy Ross made the silk flag at bottom left, with its dainty "wreath" of flowerlike white stars. The headband reads, in her own hand: "First Flag made in 1777 by Betsy Ross. This copy of the original Flag made in Dec. 1904 by Rachel Albright, aged 92 y. 6 m. Granddaughter of Betsy Ross." _Top right:_ a flag and jack of carved wood exhibiting all the characteristics of the flat, linear style of carving associated with the name of famed American folk artist John Bellamy. _Bottom right:_ music sheet of "The Triumphant Banner," a march–two step by the popular composer E. T. Paull, author of such impressively titled airs as: "Sheridan's Ride," "Custer's Last Charge," and "Battle of Gettysburg." _Opposite page:_ the crowd shown milling about on the Brooklyn Bridge on opening day, May 24, 1883, was indeed recorded from life by an artist of the period, but the giant flag shown as backdrop is a touch of fancy. Actually, this flag of thirty-six stars, smaller by far, was indeed flown on the bridge on that occasion—an interesting instance of the not-infrequent use of cherished obsolete flags on important occasions—but its actual size, 7 feet long by 4 feet wide, is nowhere near that suggested in the illustration.

Constellation to Galaxy

In the first two months of the year 1912, New Mexico and Arizona were in quick succession admitted to the Union. To amend the flag, a joint Army and Navy board headed by Admiral Dewey was assigned the task of furnishing a new design. Its suggestion was that six even rows of eight stars be used in the canton. The flag of forty-eight stars therefore was close kin to those previous Stars and Stripes whose total number of stars had permitted a similar, symmetrical pattern of aligned and equal rows, the flags of twenty, twenty-four, twenty-eight, thirty, and thirty-five stars. An all-important difference was that this time the pattern was mandatory. President William Howard Taft not only approved the board's suggestion, in February 1912, but followed up, in June and October of that year, with executive orders prescribing the exact configuration of the national flag and including the precise proportions of its devices, such as the width of the stripes and the diameter of the stars. (The exact color tints were not standardized until 1934.) As a result, although the forty-eight-star flag enjoyed the

the longest reign of all—forty-six turbulent and momentous years, at home as well as abroad—its appearance never varied. Any spontaneous popular interpretations were frowned upon after, in 1923 and 1924, patriotic associations formulated a flag etiquette which came to be known as the Flag Code. The code became Federal law in 1942.

A last original effort had been the "Great Star *cum* wreath" of the Whipple Flag of 1912 (page 121). Designer Wayne Whipple called his creation the "Peace Flag" in tribute to the global peace movement in the years preceding World War I. The same name was used a year later, unrelatedly, at a meeting of nations at The Hague, Netherlands, on August 29, 1913; prophetically, no universal Peace Flag could be decided upon, and it was agreed that each nation would have as a Peace Flag its own flag surrounded by a white border. For a time, therefore, the Peace Flag of the United States of America was the Stars and Stripes within the prescribed white frame.

One more exception to the uniformity of the forty-eight-star flag may be cited. An unusual flag of forty-eight stars was presented, on the liberation of Liège, Belgium, in 1944, to Colonel Arthur Tilghman Brice (XVIth Corps, Ninth United States Army), a great-grandson of Francis Scott Key. Like the great flag of fifteen stars and fifteen stripes celebrated by his forefather in the poem that furnished the lyrics for the American national anthem, the flag given to Colonel Brice almost one hundred and thirty years later had its canton resting on a red stripe, the so-called "war stripe"—an unexpected revival of an old American tradition. The flag is preserved in the Flag House, Baltimore.

In 1959, the admission to statehood of the giant northern territory of Alaska brought a forty-ninth star to the flag. The design of the canton of the new flag reverted to a pattern of "staggered" parallel rows (page 239). Interestingly, the occasion of Alaska's entry brought about a unique interpretation of the "American stars" in an Alaskan school contest for a state flag. The inspired, and prize-winning, creation of a thirteen-year-old Indian boy, Bennie Benson, depicted eight golden stars: the North Star, and the seven-star constellation of the Big Dipper, on a background of clear indigo blue.

When, a year later, the fiftieth star—for Hawaii—joined the flock, the "staggered" pattern was maintained. The canton now contains five parallel rows of six stars and four of five stars. The happy result is that the diagonal structure is clearly evident, creating a strikingly original effect lacking in previous flags of the quincuncial pattern but with a smaller number of stars. Admittedly, the closely pressed stars of the present flag have lost much of their individual distinctness, except at close range. A forewarning of this had been sounded by Admiral Preble, in 1872, when he exulted in "our constellation…now grown to a glorious galaxy." Just as admirable as the grandeur of its total of half a hundred stars is the astonishing versatility of the American flag, ever changeless yet ever changing, reflecting with unerring accuracy the national temper of succeeding periods: even today, though based as it is on the oldest of all American designs, the Stars and Stripes proves uncannily in tune with the mood of the age of galactic exploration.

This silk combination flag, or "flag of alliance"—American-made—displays the flags of six of the nations which participated on the side of the Allies in the First World War. Across the top: the flags of the United States and France; center row: the flags of Italy and Japan; bottom row: the flags of Great Britain and Belgium.

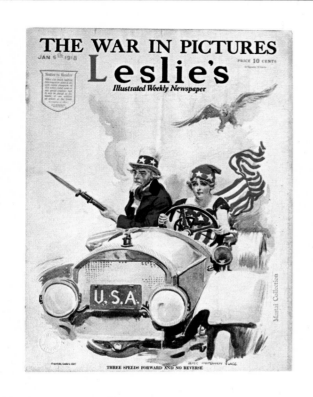

THE WAR IN PICTURES
JAN 5th 1918
Leslie's
Illustrated Weekly Newspaper
PRICE 10 CENTS

U.S.A.

THREE SPEEDS FORWARD AND NO REVERSE

Mastai Collection

Atrocity Number
APRIL 13th 1918
Leslie's
Illustrated Weekly Newspaper
PRICE 10 CENTS

MURDER   RUIN

DOING HIS BIT
OVER HALF A MILLION A WEEK
Mastai Collection

ORSON LOWELL

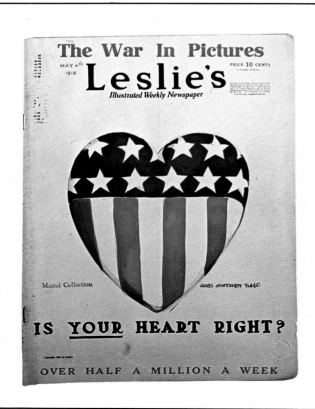

The War In Pictures
MAY 4th 1918
Leslie's
Illustrated Weekly Newspaper
PRICE 10 CENTS

Mastai Collection   JAMES MONTGOMERY FLAGG

IS YOUR HEART RIGHT?

OVER HALF A MILLION A WEEK

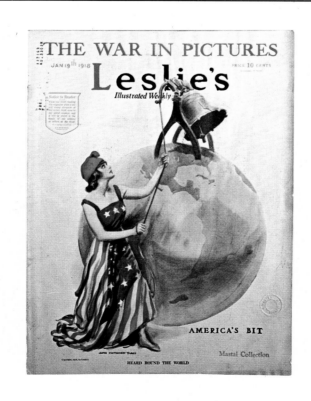

THE WAR IN PICTURES
JAN 19th 1918
Leslie's
Illustrated Weekly
PRICE 10 CENTS

AMERICA'S BIT

Mastai Collection

JAMES MONTGOMERY FLAGG

HEARD ROUND THE WORLD

Four patriotic wartime covers of LESLIE'S ILLUSTRATED WEEKLY NEWSPAPER *(<u>left and center</u>) by the well-known American illustrator James Montgomery Flagg. Lively and imaginative though each one is, the most noteworthy perhaps is the cover with "heart" motif at bottom left, where plasticity has been achieved with remarkable economy of means.*

The French silk souvenir handkerchief (1919) on the opposite page is marked by artistic and technical merit unusual in objects of this kind. The four medallions at its center are engravings. The style of the colorful garland of festooned flags is transitional between <u>art nouveau</u> and <u>art moderne</u>.

Mastai Collection

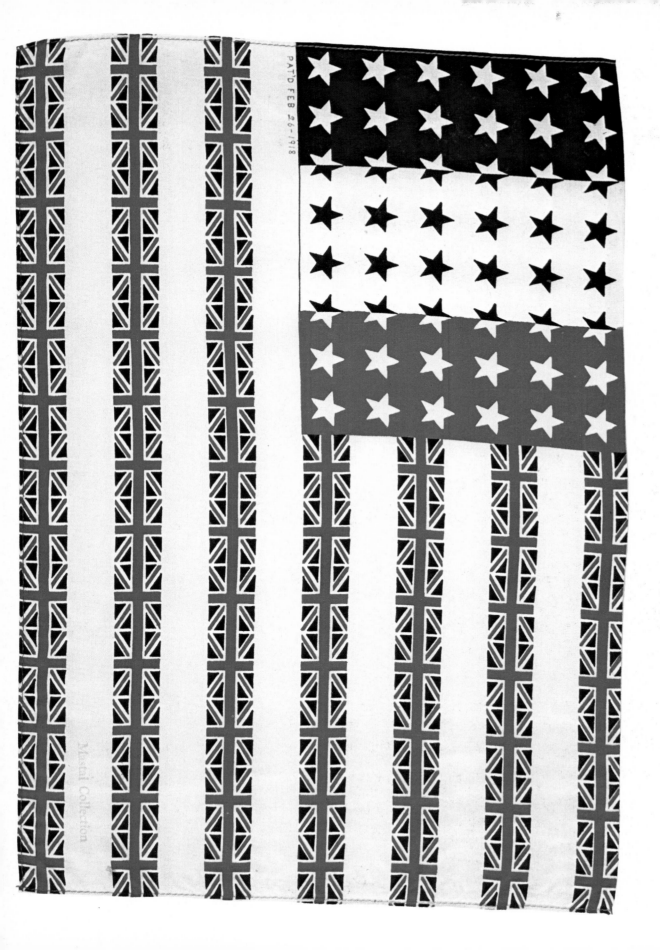

The tradition of patriotic sachets and pillow covers continued unabated in American homes during World War I. <u>Opposite page</u>, <u>top left</u>: an opened sachet with a flag of forty-eight stars. The flag is attached on three sides only; its top was left open to allow a pocket to serve as repository for mail and photographs from servicemen. <u>Top right</u>: a cross-stitched embroidered pillow with a soldier and sailor flanking a representation of a service flag. A newcomer who now joined the familiar "doughboy" and "gob" was the highly glamorous figure of the aviator, though airmen were few in number compared to members of the older services. Proud indeed was the household that was entitled to display on its service flag in the window, above the familiar blue star, the cross-shaped propeller and the word AVIATION (<u>bottom right</u>). <u>Bottom left</u>: it may have been a member of the famous Lafayette Escadrille who sent home a dainty and original sachet the embroidered cambric of which is adorned with the representation of a zooming plane whose wings consist of the American and French flags.

This "Franco-Anglo-American Flag," with American patent of February 26, 1918, is another "flag of alliance" such as that shown on page 233. Here, however, the three national flags have actually been fused instead of combined. Emphasis is, nonetheless, on the flag's American elements: the stars appear on a canton of French tricolor bands, and rows of small Union Jacks joined form the stripes. (See also the "victory flag," page 28.)

Longest lived of all Stars and Stripes, the flag of forty-eight stars was valid from July 4, 1912, to July 4, 1959. In the last year of its official existence, it was memorialized by the American artist Jasper Johns, in a painting showing it as three superimposed flags of the denomination. If the painting does not precisely symbolize the almost <u>five</u> decades of the flag's life, it does, fortuitously, suggest the flag's longevity. <u>Opposite page, left</u>: its successor, the flag of forty-nine stars, had on the contrary the minimum official life of one year's duration: July 4, 1959, to July 4, 1960. (Unofficially it had an even shorter existence—less than eight months—for though Alaska was admitted to the Union on January 3, 1959, Hawaii followed on August 21.) The design for the short-lived forty-nine-star flag reverted to a pattern of stars in "staggered" rows that had been used in the flag of forty-six stars—but in this instance there were seven rows of seven stars each.

The mammoth Stars and Stripes of fifty stars at right—the largest free-flying flag in the world—is intended to be flown, on all national holidays, on the George Washington Bridge between New York and New Jersey. Paradoxically, because of winter weather conditions it had never been possible to fly the flag on Washington's Birthday until, on February 19, 1973, with only a mild breeze blowing, the huge banner was hoisted into position. In the process, however, the folds caught on a metal extrusion, causing a long rip at the center of the flag. The flag—inadvertently emblematic of the dissensions that have wrenched the nation in recent times—remained on view in that condition until sunset, when this photograph ("The Torn Flag at Twilight") was taken by Boleslaw Mastai.

The Flag of Fifty Stars

Whatever the future may hold in store for the Stars and Stripes, it is certain that the flag of half a hundred stars began its life under extraordinary auguries. The flag at bottom, of plastic, was the first fifty-star flag to fly over the North Pole, brought there by a crew member of the atomic submarine SEA DRAGON in 1960. Less than a decade later, the world watched, breathless, while a fifty-star-flag was raised on the moon by American astronauts. The Stars and Stripes played thereby the stellar—or one might say "lunar"—role in what was certainly the scientific achievement of the millennium, the "impossible dream" to top all "impossible dreams." The occasion was also an unexpected fulfillment of what appears to have been a prophetic use of the crescent moon as a device on the "liberty flag" of Fort Moultrie (page 17, number 3), one of the earliest flags of the American patriots of the War of Independence.

A LIST OF OFFICIAL AMERICAN FLAGS AND THEIR STARS

Number of Flag	Number of Stars	Date Official	States Included and Date Admitted to Union	President(s) Serving Under the Flag	War(s) in Which the Flag Was Used
1st	13	June 14, 1777	The original thirteen founding states: Delaware; Pennsylvania; New Jersey; Georgia; Connecticut; Massachusetts; Maryland; South Carolina; New Hampshire; Virginia; New York; North Carolina; Rhode Island	George Washington	War of Independence (1775–1783)
2nd	15	May 1, 1795	Vermont (March 4, 1791); Kentucky (June 1, 1792)	George Washington; John Adams; Thomas Jefferson; James Madison; James Monroe	war with Barbary pirates (Tripoli war, 1801–1805); War of 1812 (1812–1815)
3rd	20	April 13, 1818	Tennessee (June 1, 1796); Ohio (February 19, 1803); Louisiana (April 30, 1812); Indiana (December 11, 1816); Mississippi (December 10, 1817)	James Monroe	
4th	21	July 4, 1819	Illinois (December 3, 1818)	James Monroe	
5th	23	July 4, 1820	Alabama (December 14, 1819); Maine (March 15, 1820)	James Monroe	
6th	24	July 4, 1822	Missouri (August 10, 1821)	James Monroe; John Quincy Adams; Andrew Jackson	
7th	25	July 4, 1836	Arkansas (June 15, 1836)	Andrew Jackson; Martin Van Buren	
8th	26	July 4, 1837	Michigan (January 26, 1837)	Martin Van Buren; William Henry Harrison; John Tyler; James K. Polk	
9th	27	July 4, 1845	Florida (March 3, 1845)	James K. Polk	Mexican War (1846–1848)
10th	28	July 4, 1846	Texas (December 29, 1845)	James K. Polk	Mexican War
11th	29	July 4, 1847	Iowa (December 28, 1846)	James K. Polk	Mexican War
12th	30	July 4, 1848	Wisconsin (May 29, 1848)	James K. Polk; Zachary Taylor; Millard Fillmore	
13th	31	July 4, 1851	California (September 9, 1850)	Millard Fillmore; Franklin Pierce; James Buchanan	
14th	32	July 4, 1858	Minnesota (May 11, 1858)	James Buchanan	
15th	33	July 4, 1859	Oregon (February 14, 1859)	James Buchanan; Abraham Lincoln	Civil War (1861–1865)
16th	34	July 4, 1861	Kansas (January 29, 1861)	Abraham Lincoln	Civil War
17th	35	July 4, 1863	West Virginia (June 20, 1863)	Abraham Lincoln; Andrew Johnson	Civil War
18th	36	July 4, 1865	Nevada (October 31, 1864)	Andrew Johnson	
19th	37	July 4, 1867	Nebraska (March 1, 1867)	Andrew Johnson; Ulysses S. Grant; Rutherford B. Hayes	
20th	38	July 4, 1877	Colorado (August 1, 1876)	Rutherford B. Hayes; James Garfield; Chester Alan Arthur; Grover Cleveland; Benjamin Harrison	
21st	43	July 4, 1890	North Dakota (November 2, 1889); South Dakota (November 2, 1889); Montana (November 8, 1889); Washington (November 11, 1889); Idaho (July 3, 1890)	Benjamin Harrison	
22nd	44	July 4, 1891	Wyoming (July 10, 1890)	Benjamin Harrison; Grover Cleveland	
23rd	45	July 4, 1896	Utah (January 4, 1896)	Grover Cleveland; William McKinley; Theodore Roosevelt	Spanish-American War (1898)
24th	46	July 4, 1908	Oklahoma (November 16, 1907)	Theodore Roosevelt; William Howard Taft	
25th	48	July 4, 1912	New Mexico (January 6, 1912); Arizona (February 14, 1912)	William Howard Taft; Woodrow Wilson; Warren G. Harding; Calvin Coolidge; Herbert Hoover; Franklin D. Roosevelt; Harry S. Truman; Dwight D. Eisenhower	World War I (1917–1918); World War II (1941–1945); Korean War (1950–1953)
26th	49	July 4, 1959	Alaska (January 3, 1959)	Dwight D. Eisenhower	
27th	50	July 4, 1960	Hawaii (August 21, 1959)	Dwight D. Eisenhower; John F. Kennedy; Lyndon Johnson; Richard Nixon	Vietnam War (1961–1973)

A LIST OF SOURCES AND CREDITS

Except as specified below, all flags and related items in this book are from the Mastai Collection, with special photography by Boleslaw Mastai and additional photography by Robert Brandau Associates.

THE AMERICAN STRIPES

North Carolina Militia Flag (detail, page 14; shown in full on page 39), courtesy of North Carolina Department of Archives and History, Raleigh; *Flag of the Philadelphia Troop of Light Horse* (page 21), courtesy of the Officers and Gentlemen of the First Troop Philadelphia City Cavalry; *Flag of the 2nd Light Dragoons, Continental Line* (page 21), courtesy of the Smithsonian Institution, Washington, D.C.; *Flag of "Sullivan's Life Guard"* (page 22), courtesy of the Rhode Island Historical Society, Providence, photograph by E. Andrew Mowbray; SIEGE OF YORKTOWN *watercolor* (page 22), from the Simcoe Papers, Colonial Williamsburg Foundation, Williamsburg, Virginia; *Banner of the Cincinnati* (page 24), property of the New York State Society of the Cincinnati, courtesy of the Society of the Cincinnati, Headquarters and Museum, Anderson House, Washington, D.C., photograph by Henry B. Beville; *Flag of the Scituate Guards* (page 24), courtesy of the Rhode Island Historical Society, photograph by E. Andrew Mowbray; *George Washington portrait banner* (page 27), courtesy of the Smithsonian Institution.

THE FIRST STARS

Stark Flag (page 30), courtesy of The Bennington Museum, Bennington, Vermont; *Flag of the Rhode Island Company of the United Train of Artillery* (page 33), courtesy of the Rhode Island Historical Society, Providence, photograph by E. Andrew Mowbray; *Pulaski Banner* (page 34), courtesy of the Maryland Historical Society, Baltimore, photograph by Hughes Co.; *Hulbert Flag* (page 34), courtesy of the Suffolk County Historical Society Museum, Riverhead, New York; *Bennington Flag* (page 35), courtesy of The Bennington Museum; *Beauvais tapestry* (page 36), courtesy of the National Trust, (Osterley Park) England; *Seutter and Mondhare flag sheets (details)* (page 36), courtesy of the John Carter Brown Library, Brown University, Providence; *Easton Flag* (page 39), courtesy of the Easton Area Public Library, photography by the Jack and Jill Studio, Easton, Pennsylvania.

A NEW CONSTELLATION

Flag Resolution (page 45), from the "Papers of the Continental Congress," courtesy of the Center for the Documentary Study of the American Revolution, National Archives and Records Service, Washington, D.C.; *Baumann map* (page 45), from the I. N. Phelps Stokes Collection, The New York Public Library, Astor, Lenox and Tilden Foundations; THE SURRENDER OF GENERAL BURGOYNE *painting* (page 45), courtesy of the Yale University Art Gallery, New Haven; *Buell map* (page 48), courtesy of the New Jersey Historical Society, Newark; *Fort Independence Flag* (page 48), courtesy of the Massachusetts Art Commission, photograph by Mark Sexton; *Fort Hill Flag* (page 50), courtesy of the Smithsonian Institution, Washington, D.C.; *Fifteen-star flag* (top, page 52), courtesy of the Calvert Distillers Company; *Star-Spangled Banner* (page 53), courtesy of the Smithsonian Institution.

FLAG OF THE SEAS

Texel paintings of the ALLIANCE *and* SERAPIS *flags* (page 59), courtesy of the Chicago Historical Society; *Augsburg flag sheet* (page 61), courtesy of The Mariners Museum, Newport News, Virginia; SOUTH CAROLINA *watercolor* (page 65), courtesy of the Peabody Museum at Salem, Massachusetts, photograph by Mark Sexton; UNITED STATES *painting* (page 69), courtesy of Warren Sturgis, New York City; *Twenty-five-star "Great Star" flag* (page 74), courtesy of The Huntington Historical Society, Huntington, Long Island; BENMORE *figurehead* (page 78), courtesy of The Mariners Museum.

THE EAGLE AND THE FLAG

Frémont Flag (page 82), courtesy of the Southwest Museum, Los Angeles; *U.S. 1st Infantry Regiment national color* (page 88), courtesy of the West Point Museum, U.S. Military Academy, photograph by A. T. Murphy, Jr.; VIEW OF THE CANNON HOUSE AND WHARF *painting* (page 89), courtesy of The Dietrich Brothers Americana Corporation; *Nashville Battalion flag* (page 89), courtesy of the Smithsonian Institution, Washington, D.C.; *Scene at Fort Union drawing* (page 93), courtesy of the Thomas Gilcrease Institute of American History and Art, Tulsa; *Flag of the 4th Indiana Volunteers* (page 93), courtesy of the Smithsonian Institution; *Headquarters flag, Department of the Cumberland* (page 95), courtesy of the West Point Museum, U.S. Military Academy.

THE STARRY FLOWER

Pershing flag (or thirty-four-star "Great Star" flag) (page 98), courtesy of the Smithsonian Institution, Washington, D.C.; *"Pentagon flag"* (top, page 104), courtesy of The Star-Spangled Banner Flag House, Baltimore; *Whaling ship painting* (bottom, page 104), courtesy of Mrs. Barbara Johnson, Princeton, N. J.; *Commodore Perry's ship in Japan* and *Triptych of Perry and his men in Yokohama paintings* (pages 106 and 107), courtesy of the Library of Congress, Washington, D.C.

STARS IN THE STORM

Fort Sumter garrison flag (page 125), courtesy of the National Geographic Society, photograph by Dick Burbage, (c) National Geographic Society; *23rd Army Corps national color* (page 142), courtesy of the West Point Museum, U.S. Military Academy; *Kohn flag presented to Lincoln* (page 145), courtesy of Joan W. Saltzstein, Milwaukee; *"Old Glory"* (page 153), courtesy of the Smithsonian Institution, Washington, D.C.; *Lincoln mourning-train photograph* (pages 136 and 137), courtesy of the Ostendorf Collection, Dayton, Ohio.

THE FLAG IN DAILY LIFE

"Flag pasture-gate" (page 177), courtesy of the Museum of American Folk Art, New York City, gift of Herbert W. Hemphill, Jr.

THE TRIUMPHANT BANNER

Opening of the Brooklyn Bridge drawing (page 229), courtesy of The Bettmann Archive, Inc., New York City.

CONSTELLATION TO GALAXY

THREE FLAGS *painting* (page 238), from the collection of Mr. and Mrs. Burton Tremaine, Meriden, Connecticut; *Fifty-star submarine flag* (page 240), courtesy of The Mariners Museum, Newport News, Virginia; *Astronauts and flag on moon* (page 241), courtesy of N.A.S.A., Washington, D.C.

Index

Page numbers in italics indicate illustrations.

A

Act to Establish the Flag (1818), 29, 51, 54, 68; "Third Flag," 54, 100, 123, 160
Adams, John, 29, 47, 60, 64, 96, 105
Adams, John Quincy, 86
Alabama state flag, *136*, 136
Alaska, flag celebrating entry, 232, 238, *239*
Alaska state flag, 232
Albright, Rachel, flag made by, *228*, 228
"All-Seeing Eye," *see* eye motif
Allen, Edward J., 29
Alliance Flag, *59*, 59, 64, 68
"America" (personifications), *23*, 23, 32, *84*, 84, 85, *196*, 196, *198–9*, 198–9; *see also* "Columbia"; "Liberty"
America (yacht) Flag, 80, *81*
Anglo-American flag, 226
Apotheosis of Benjamin Franklin and George Washington, *23*, 23, 32
"Arctic Flag," *78*, 79, 79; *see also* North Pole
assassinated presidents, flag used for, 154, *154–5*, *191*, 191, 192
Augsburg flag sheet, 59, *61*, 61
Australia, flag of, 41

B

Bancel, Madam, flag made by, *24*, 24
Barnes, R. L., 77
Barry, Capt. John, 69
Barton, Thomas, 47
"Battle Flag," *see* "Southern Cross"
Baumann, Maj. Sebastian, map of Yorktown, *45*, 45
Belgium, flag of, *233*, 233
Bellamy, John, 228
Benmore figurehead, *78*, 78
Bennington Flag, *35*, 35, 37, 62, 68
Benson, Bennie, 232
Bernard, Louis, 116
"Betsy Ross" pattern, *see* star patterns, "wreath"
"Bible flags," 137
Blaine, James G.: portrait of, *208*, 208; name on flag, *209*
blue, use of, 25, 43, 109; *see also* stars, color of; stripes, color of
Bonhomme Richard Flag, 64, 160, 164
"Bonnie Blue Flag," 130, 138
Botta, Carlo, *History of the War of Independence*, 20
Bragg, Capt. H. M., 154
Brice, Col. Arthur Tilghman, 232
Brooklyn Bridge, opening of, 228, *229*

"Brotherhood of America" poster-diploma, *227*, 227
Bryan, William Jennings, poster of, *212*, 212
Budington, John, *View of the Cannon House and Wharf*, *89*, 89
Buell, Abel, map of the United States, 45, *48*, 48
Bunker Hill flags, 16, *204*, 204, 226
business and advertising (and the flag), *183*, 183, *192*, 192, *203*, 203
Bute, John Stuart, Lord, 63
Butler, Gen. Benjamin F., 133
Buxton, Charles, 40

C

California, flag celebrating entry, 172, *173*
Cannon, John, 89
cards, envelopes, and stationery (and the flag), 140, *141*, *150–1*, 150–1, *183*, 183, *192*, 192, *203*, 203, 223
Carnegie, Andrew, 226
Casey, Lt. E. W., 222
Centennial, *see* First Centennial
children (and the flag), 137, *183*, 183, *200*, 200, *201*, *202*, 202, *203*, 23
Chinese art, 92, *93*, 94, *95*, *194*, 194
Civil War: commemorative items and mementoes, *78*, 78, 130, 140, *141*, *150–1*, 150–1, *180*, 180, 192; G.A.R. plaque, *194*, 194; in music, 126, *127*, *135*, 135, *196*, 196, *206*, 206, 228; personifications, 196, *197*, 197; pictorial record, 126, *127*, *140*, 140, *142–3*, 143, *144*, 144, *154*, 154
Civil War flags, 62, *78*, 78, 94, *95*, 96, 123–4, 142, *142–3*, 143, *145*, 145, *176*, 176; Confederacy, 130, *134–41*, 135, 137, 138, 140, 153, 226; miniature flags, 137, 188, *188–9*, *200*, 200, *201*; Union, *125*, 125, *126*, 126, *128*, 128, *129*, 130, 133, 137, *144*, 144, *146–7*, *148*, *149*, 149, 153
Cleveland, Grover, 226
Coast Guard and Customs Flag, 19, *28*, 28, 75, 96
Cockley, Thomas, 119
colonial flags, 16, *17*, 17, *18*, 18, 19; *see also* Revolutionary War
Colorado, flag celebrating entry, *80*, 80, 160
"Columbia" (personifications), *40*, 40, *71*, 71, *78*, 78, *196*, 198; *see also* "America"; "Liberty"
Columbian Exposition (Chicago, 1893), 223
"The Confederate Flag" (poem), *141*
Confederate flags, 130, *134–41*, 135, 137, 138, 140, 153, 226
"Conquered Banner" ("Flag of the Lost Cause"), 130, 140, *141*; *see also*

"Southern Cross"
Constitution, 65, 68
Cook, John & Charles, wallpaper, *190*, 191
Cowpens Flag, 39, 44; *see also* star patterns, "Third Maryland"
"Crosses and Stripes," *65*, 65; *see also* Grand Union Flag
Cross of St. Andrew, *see* star patterns, Cross of St. Andrew
Cross of St. George, 15–16, *17*, 62, 68, 70, *109*, 109, 172, *173*; *see also* star patterns, Cross of St. George
Cuba, flag of, *224*, 224
Currier & Ives prints, 126, *127*, *140*, 140, *197*, 197, *204*, 204
Custer. Col. George, 160, 222, 228

D

Davis, Jefferson, 124, 140; portrait, *141*
Davis, Capt. R. C., 79
Democratic Convention hall (1868), *210*, 211
Department of the Cumberland Flag, 94, 95
Desmoulins, Camille, 25
Dewey, Adm. George, *203*, 203, *219*, 219, 226, 231
Dimitry, John, 140, *141*
Dix, Gen. John Adams, 126, *127*
Dodge family, 121
Downey, Sarah, 112
Driver, Capt. Stephen, 153
Donnelly, T. J., 29
Durand, Sir Henry Mortimer, 193

E

eagle: adoption as national bird, 85; Chinese embroidery, 92, *93*, 94, *95*; Filipino mat, *219*, 219; flags, colors, and "standards of the eagle," 19, *28*, 28, *72–3*, 73, *75*, *84*, 84, 85–6, *88–93*, 88, 89, 91, 92, 94, 96, *196*, 196; French medal, 85; G.A.R. plaque, *194*; Great Seal, 28, 85, 86, 100; heraldry, *84*, 84, *89*, 89, 94, *95*; Indian art, *97*, 97; in music, *94*, 94, 96, *184*; on passport, 86, 96; symbolism and use of, 21, 83, 85, *87*, 87, 100
"Early American History" coverlet, *178*, 178
East India Company flag, 20
Easton Flag, *39*, 39
Elliott, Jane, 16
Ellsworth, Col. Elmer E., lithograph, *140*, 140
"Emblem of America," *84*, 84
English, William Hayden, 38
Eric the Red, 15–16

Eutaw Flag, 16
Everett, Edward, 130
eye motif, *34*, 34, 37, 193

F

Fairburn, John, 84
Fairlie, Maj. James, 24
fans (and the flag), *165*, 165, *170*, 170, *195*, 195, *224*, 224, *227*, 227
Field, Cyrus W., 226
First Centennial, commemorative items and mementoes, *159*, 159, *165*, 165, *170*, 170, *171*, 171, *183*, 183, *194*, 194
First Centennial flags, *18*, 18, 70, 105, *116*, 116, *118*, 119, *156*, 157, *158*, 158, *159*, 159, 160, *162*, 162, *163*, 163, 164, *166–7*, 167, *171*, 171, *172*, 172, *173*, *183*, 183, 189, 189, *194*, 194, *202*, 202, 208, *209*
"First Flag," 172, 178, 227, 228, *see also* stars, number of, (13)
1st Infantry Regiment colors, *88*, 88
flag (and flag devices and motifs) uses in daily life, *174*, 175, *180*, 180, *181*, 181, *190*, 191, *193*, 193, *195*, 195, *202*, 202, *203*, 203, *210*, 211, 223, *234*, 234; *see also* business and advertising; cards, envelopes, and stationery; fans; jewelry; metal artifacts; music; politics; textiles, tapestry, and needlework; woodcarving
flag charts or sheets, 16, *36*, 36, 59, *61*, 61, *75*, 75, *77*, 77
Flag Code, flag laws, and flag etiquette, 105, 109, 124, 168, 175, 211, 231, 232
Flag Day, 215
Flagg, James Montgomery, *234*, 234
flag legends: Bonhomme Richard Flag, 64, 160, 164; Ross, Betsy, as creator, 15, 32, 37, 44, 47, 164, 187, *203*, 203, 228; Washington, George, as designer, 32, 37, 47, 164; Washington family coat-of-arms, as basis, 20, *21*, 21, 32, 37, 164
"flaglets," 137, *159*, 159, *183*, 183, *200*, 200; *see also* miniature flags
"flag of alliance," 226, *233*, 233, *237*, 237; *see also* "International Flag"
"Flag of All Nations," 171
"Flag of the Lost Cause" ("Conquered Banner"), 130, 140, *141*; *see also* "Southern Cross"
Flag Resolution (1777), 25, 32, 41, 43, *45*, 45, 47, 49, 58, 59, 60, 101, 114; *see also* "First Flag"
flag resolution of 1795, 29, 49; "Second Flag," 49, 53
"Flags of the Principal Nations of the World" (chart), *77*, 77
Fort Hill Flag, 29, *50*, 50
Fort Independence Flag, *48*, 48
Fort Keogh Flag, *222*, 222

Fort McHenry and Star-Spangled Banner, 29, 49, 52, *53*, 99, 160, 223, 232
Fort Moultrie Flag, *17*, 17, 19, 240
Fort Sumter, 130, 133; flags, 70, 112, *125*, 125, *154*, 154
Fort Union Flag, 92, *93*
"Four-Cornered Flag," 154, *163*, 163
4th Indiana Volunteers flag, 92, *93*, 94
France: flags of, 25, *40*, 40, 61, *223*, 233, 234, *235*, 237, 237; flag sheets, *36*, 36, *75*, 75; tapestry and textiles, *36*, 36, 234, *235*, *236*, 237
"Franco-Anglo-American Flag," *237*, 237
Frank Leslie's Illustrated History of the Civil War, 126, *127*, *144*, 144, *154*, 154
Franklin, Benjamin, 23, 29, 47, 64, 85, 87, 96, 164; painting of, *23*
Frémont Flag (John C. Frémont), *82*, 83, 92, 96

G

Garfield, James A., band, *211*, 211
George II, King, 83
George III, King, 20, 63
George Washington Bridge flag, *239*, 239
Germany: flag of, *180*, 180; flag sheet, *36*, 36
"Gildersleeve Meteor" (S. Gildersleeve), 114, *114–15*
Grand Army of the Republic plaque, *194*, 194
Grand Union Flag, *18*, 18, 20, 25, 58, 65, 68, 160
Grant, Gen. Ulysses S., 208, *212*, 212
Great Britain: flags of, 15–16, *17*, 20, *40*, 41, 68, 109, 193, *226*, *233*, 233, *237*, 237; textiles, *23*, 23, 32, *40*, 40
"Great Double-Wreath Flag," *118*, 119, 164
"Great Flower," *see* star patterns, "Great Flower"
Great Seal, 28, 47, 85, 86, 89, 100, 121, *230*, 231
"Great Star," 100; *see also* star patterns, "Great Star"
Green, Valentine, 23
green, symbolism and use of, 16, 25, 58; *see also* "Pine Tree Flag"; Stark Flag
"Green Tree Flag," 16, 58

H

Hall, Charles B., 140
Hamilton, Gen. Schuyler, 100
Hamilton, 70
Hancock, Winfield Scott, 38
Harper's Magazine vignettes, *142–3*, 143
Harper's Weekly picture, *159*, 159
Harrison, Benjamin, 191, 208; textile, *191*; name band, *209*
Hayes, Patrick, 69
Hayes Arctic Expedition flag, *78*, *79*, 79
heraldry: eagle, *84*, 84, *89*, 89, 94, *95*;

stripes, *35*, 35, *36*, 36, , 40, 52, *59*, 59, 92, 92, *93*; *see also* star patterns, Cross of St. Andrew, Cross of St. George, quincuncial; stars
Herschel, William, 32
Hobart, Garret A., portrait, *211*, 211
Holmes, Oliver Wendell, 99
Hopkinson, Francis, 47, 49, 60
Horn, Capt. Abraham, 39
"Hour-Glass Flag," *116*, 116, 157, 172, *173*
Hubbard family, 52
Hulbert Flag, *34*, 34, 70, 125

I

Icard, Louis, 199
"Independent Order of Odd Fellows" medal, *193*, 193
Indians and Indian art, 43, 83, *84*, 89, *90–1*, 90–1, 92, *93*, 96, *97*, 97, *195*, 195, 222, 226
inscriptions, *see* writing
"International Flag," *162*, 162, 171
international flags, *see* "flag of alliance"; "Flag of All Nations"; Peace Flags
Iowa, flag celebrating entry, 172, *173*
Irvine Flag (William Neill Irvine), 70, 112, *112–13*, 125
Italy, flag of, *233*, 233

J

Jackson, Andrew, 223
Japan: art, *104*, 104, *106*, *107*, 107, *165*, 165, *180*, 180, *233*, 233; flags of, *180*, 180, *233*, 233
Jefferson, Thomas, 44, 47
Jersey City, railroad depot flags, 126, *127*, *146–7*, 149
jewelry (and the flag), *71*, 71, 77, *194*, 194, *211*, 211
Johns, Jasper, painting, *238*, 238
Jones, John Paul, 25, 58, 59, 60, 64, 68

K

Kansas, flag celebrating entry, *119*, 119, 160
Kathleen, *76*, 76
Kellogg, E. B. and E. C., 200
Kennedy, John F., 154
Keogh, Capt. Myles W., 222
Key, Francis Scott, "Star-Spangled Banner," 29, 49, 99, 232
Key, Francis Scott, III, 203
Kilby, John, 64
Kingsboro Flag, 92, 92
Know-Nothings, 27; flags, *26*, 27, 191
Knox, Gen., 86
Kohn, Abraham, 142, *143*
Kościuszko, Thaddeus, 85
Ku Klux Klan belt buckle, *180*, 180
Kurz, Rudolf Friedrich, drawing, 92, *93*

L

Lafayette, Marquis de, 25, 29, 223
"lapel flags," *189*, 189
Laurens, Henry, 64
Lebarbier, J.-J.-F., the elder, 36
Lee, Arthur, 64
legends about the flag, *see* flag legends
L'Enfant, Maj. Pierre, 46
Leslie, Frank, *see Frank Leslie's Illustrated History of the Civil War*
Leslie's Illustrated Weekly Newsletter covers, *234*, 234
"Liberty" (personifications), 196, *197*, 197, *198–9*, 198–9; *see also* "America"; "Columbia"
"liberty flags," *17*, 17, 19, 240
Lincoln, Abraham, 94, 123, 125, 142, 149, 154; on belt buckle, *122*, *154*; on pamphlet, *212*
"living flag," 226
Logan, John A.: portrait, *208*, 208; name on flag, *209*
Lotos Club (N.Y.) flag, *193*, 193
Louis XVI, King, 36
Lundy, Rev. J. P., 126
"Lyra Flag," 96, 105

M

Magnus, Charles, 126
Markoe, Abraham, 20, 21, 39; Flag, *21*
Marschall, Nicola, 135
"Mary Eliza" pennant, *72–3*, 73, 79
Masonic influence, 37, 47; on flags and banners, *34*, 34, *35*, 35, 37, 62, 114
McClellan, Maj. Gen. George, 200, 206; flags, *206–7*; music sheet, *206*
McKinley, William, 115, 164, 192, *211*, 226; portrait, *211*
McNamara Flag (Matthew McNamara), *161*, 161
"medallion" flags, *see* star patterns, "medallion"
metal artifacts (and the flag), *122*, 123, *154*, 154, *180*, 180
"Meteor Flag," 41; *see also* "Gildersleeve Meteor"
Metropolitan Museum of Art (N.Y.), 212
Mexican War flags, 62, 92, *93*, 96
Millard, Harrison, 29
Minerva Flag, *66*, 66, *67*
mniature flags, 137, *159*, 159, *183*, 183, 188, *188–9*, 189, 193, *200*, 200, *201*, *202*, 202, 220, *220–1*
"Miss America," *see* "America"
"Miss Liberty," *see* "Liberty"
Mondhare flag chart, *36*, 36
Monitor, *78*, 78
Monroe, James, 68
moon, flag planted on, 240, *241*
Morse, Samuel F. B., 124

mottoes, *see* writing
Moultrie Flag (Col. William Moultrie), *17*, 17, 19, 240
mourning flag, 154, *154–5*
music, patriotic, *27*, 27, 29, *184–5*, 185, *186–7*, 187, *196*, 196, *204*, 204, 223, 226, *228*, 228; Civil War, 126, *127*, *135*, 135, *196*, *206*, 206, 228; eagle celebrated in, *94*, 94, 96, *184*; "Star-Spangled Banner," 29, 49, 99, 232

N

Nashville Battalion flag, *89*, 89, 94, 138
national color, oldest numbered, *88*, 88
naval and merchant marine flags and ensigns, 19, 25, *28*, 28, 41, 51, 54, *56*, 57–65 *passim*, *59*, 61, 62, 63, 65, 66, 67, 67, 68, 69, 69, 70, *72–8*, 73, 75–9 *passim*, 85, 96, 99, *126*, 126, *182*, 183, *190*, 191
Netherlands: flags of, 58; flag sheet (1693), 16
Newcomb Flag, 133
New England Worsted Company (Saxonville, Mass.), 128, 133
New York Public Schools centennial flag, *189*, 189
New York State League ribbon, *211*, 211
New Zealand, flag of, 41
Niagara ensign, 226
"nine," symbolism and use of, 19, 63; *see also* stripes, number of, (9)
Nini, Jean-Baptiste, 23
North Carolina Militia Flag, *14*, 15, *39*, 39
North Pole, flags planted at, 226, *240*, 240

O

"Old Abe," *94*, 94, 96
"Old Glory," *153*, 153
"Open-Center Flag," *131*, 131
Oregon, flags celebrating entry, *159*, 159, 172, *173*
"Our Colors" (print), *200*, 200

P

Paine, Tom, 19
"Palmetto Flag," 130
Pan-American Exposition (Buffalo, 1901), 192; postcard, *192*
paper flags, *188*, 188, *189*, 189, 193, *202*, 202
"Parenthesis Flag," *115*, 115
patriotism, personifications of: female, *23*, 23, 32, *40*, 40, *71*, 71, *78*, 78, *84*, 84, 85, 196, *197*, 197, *198–9*, 198–9, 214, *215*; Uncle Sam, *183*, 183, *191*, 191, *202*, 202
Paull, E. T., 223, 226, 228, 228
"peace flags" (Civil War), 124
Peace Flags (international), 232; *see also* Whipple Flag

Peale, Charles Willson, 39, 44
Peary, Robert E., 226
"Pelican Flag," 130
Pennsylvania, state arms of, 86
Perry, Comm. Matthew C., 107; ship paintings, 106-7
Pershing, Gen. John J., flag, 98, 99
Peters, Richard, 60
Philadelphia Troop of Light Horse standard, 20, 21, 21, 39
Philippines, flag of, 219, 219
Phippen, John, watercolor, 65, 65
"Pine Tree Flag," 17, 17, 19, 130
politics (and the flag), 189, 189, 204, 204-13, 206, 208, 211, 212; see also writing
portraits on flags, 26, 27, 27, 140, 141, 158, 168, 169, 191, 192, 192, 208, 208, 209
Portsmouth (R.I.), town seal of, 32
Preble, Adm. George Henry, 25, 70, 71, 77, 124, 130, 232
"Prisoner's Flag," 62, 62
Providence (R.I.), town seal of, 32
Pulaski Banner (Gen. Count Casimir Pulaski), 34, 34, 37
Puritans, and "red ensign," 16, 17, 17

R

rattlesnake: symbolism and use of, 19-20, 140, 141; flags, devices, ensigns, and standards, 17, 17, 20, 22, 23, 33, 33, 58, 85, 130, 196, 196
"red ensign," 15-16, 17, 17, 19, 20, 41
Red Star of Russia, China, 41
Reed, Col. Joseph, 58
Reid, Capt. Samuel C., 51, 60, 68, 86, 100, 124
Remington, Frederic, 222
Reprisal Flag, 22, 23
Revenue Cutters Flag, 19, 28, 28, 73, 96
Revolutionary War flags, 17, 17, 19-20, 21, 21, 22, 23, 23, 25, 29, 32, 33, 33, 34, 34, 35, 35, 39, 39, 41, 43, 44, 44, 45, 45, 47, 58, 59, 59, 62, 62, 63, 63, 66, 66, 240
Rhode Island: militia and regiment flags of, 22, 23, 24, 24, 32, 33, 33; seals, 32
Rhode Island Scituate Guards flag, 24, 24
"Rippled Flag," 177, 177
Robertson, Lt. S. C., 222

S

Scott, Edith, 202
Scott, Gen. Winfield, 100; portrait, 204, 204
Sea Dragon Flag, 240
"Second Flag," 49, 53
2nd Light Dragoons, Continental Line, flags, 21, 21
Serapis Flag, 59, 59, 60, 62, 64, 68
service flag, 237, 237
Seutter, Mattheus, flag sheet, 36, 36
Seymour, Horatio, motto, 212, 213
Sherman, Mrs. Roger, 86

Shifler, George, 27; lithograph, 27
Simcoe, Lt. Col. John Graves, watercolor, 22-3, 23
Simitière, Eugène Pierre du, 47
"Sixth Regiment of Massachusetts Volunteers" picture, 126, 127
Society of the Cincinnati banner, 24, 24, 46
"Sons of Liberty," 19
Sousa, John Philip, "Stars and Stripes Forever," 186, 223
South Carolina (warship) Flag, 65, 65
South Carolina navy flag, 23, 23, 39
"Southern Cross" ("Battle Flag"), 130, 136, 137; see also "Conquered Banner" ("Flag of the Lost Cause")
Spanish-American War, commemorative items and mementoes, 187, 223, 224, 224
Spanish-American War flags, 218, 218, 219, 224, 224, 225, 225, 226
Spear, John, 66
Spencer, Lilly Martin, "Pic Nic of the Fourth of July...," 200, 200
Sprengel Flag (Matthias Sprengel), 59, 59, 61
Stafford, Sarah Smith, 164
Stagg, Lt. John, Jr., 24
"Stainless Banner," see "White Man's Flag"
star patterns: "arch," 35, 35, 37, 62, 62; "battalion," see "phalanx" below; "Betsy Ross," see "wreath" below; circle, 28, 44, 45, 70, and see also "wreath" below; "cross," 34, 34, 70, 125, 125; Cross of St. Andrew (saltire), 62, 68, 109, 109, 116, 116, 130, 172, 173; Cross of St. George, 62, 68, 70, 109, 109, 172, 173; "diamond," 70, 112, 112-13, 125, 125; "global" (or "spherical"), 164, 172, 173, 208, 209; "Great Flower," 101, 108, 109, 109, 111, 111, 181, 181; "Great Star" (or "Great Luminary"), 51, 54, 54, 68, 70, 74, 75, 98, 99-100, 101, 101, 102, 103, 103, 105, 110, 111, 121, 126, 127, 154, 154-5, 181, 181, 208, 209, 232; "kinetic," 101, 101, 105, 110, 111, 115, 115; lyre, 96, 105; "medallion," 105, 118, 119, 120, 121, 160, 212; oval, 28, 46, 46, 52, 52, 68, and see also "wreath" below; "parenthesis," 115, 115; "pentagon," 103, 104, 104; "phalanx" (or "battalion"), 105, 123, 126, 126, 130, 131, 131, 142, 143, 152, 152, 172, 172; quincuncial, 49, 59, 64, 68, 76, 132, 132, 149, 149, 232, and see also "staggered" below; saltire, see Cross of St. Andrew above; "scatter," 56, 57, 76, 76, 128, 128; "spherical," see "global" above; "square frame" (or "square formation"), 45, 45, 68, 71, 71, 77, 77, 78, 78, 119, 131, 163, 163; "staggered," 49, 54, 68, 80, 81, 172, 173, 218, 219, 225, 225, 232, 238, 239, and see also quincuncial above; "Third Maryland," 42, 43,

44, 44, 148, 149, 182, 183; "wreath" (or "Betsy Ross"), 44, 44, 52, 68, 99, 105, 130, 134, 135, 135, 137, 137, 138, 138, 164, 178, 178, 194, 194, 228, 228; "double-wreath," 80, 80, 105, 118, 119, 145, 148, 149, 159, 159, 161, 161, 164, 172, 173, 194, 194, 212, 213; "triple-wreath," 105
Stark, Gen. John, 31, 35; Flag, 30, 31
stars, 29, 41, 43; diameter regulated, 231; pointing in same direction, 101; symbolism of, 31-32; see also flag (and flag devices and motifs); Great Seal
stars, color of: blue, 14, 22, 23, 28, 28, 38, 38, 39, 39, 41, 136, 137; gold, 41, 144, 144, 200, 200, 206, 206, 207; red, 72-3, 73
stars, number of, reflecting current number of states in Union (or Confederacy), 41, 49, 105, 160; (1), 138; (7), 130, 134, 135, 135, 140, 140; (11), 41, 130, 135, 135, 136, 137, 138, 138; (12), 138, 139; (13), 28, 28, 30, 33, 34, 36, 38, 38, 39, 39, 40, 40, 41, 42, 43, 44, 44, 46, 46, 48, 49, 59, 62, 62-6 passim, 63, 65, 66, 68, 71, 71, 78, 101, 101, 130, 137, 148, 149, 172, 178, 178, 182, 183, 227, 227, 228, 228; (15), 40, 40, 44, 44, 49, 50, 50, 51, 52, 52, 53, 71, 71, 79, 99, 232; (17), 52, 52; (18), 78, 79, 79; (20), 20, 51, 54, 54, 55, 55, 100, 160, 231; (21), 148, 149; (23), 148, 149; (24), 153, 153, 231; (25), 75, 95, 176, 176, 188, 188; (26), 82, 90-1, 91, 92, 92, 102, 103, 103, 114, 114-15, 197, 197; (28), 231; (29), 172, 173; (30), 70, 100, 231; (31), 56, 57, 70, 76, 76, 77, 77, 104, 172, 173; (33), 111, 111, 112, 112, 115, 120, 121, 125, 128, 128, 159, 159, 172, 173, 189, 189; (34), 98, 99, 108, 109, 109, 111, 111, 119, 119, 126, 126, 128, 129, 131, 131, 145, 145, 160, 188, 188, 204, 205; (35), 110, 111, 143, 143, 144, 144, 146-7, 149, 231; (36), 116, 117, 132, 132, 133, 142, 142, 152, 152, 154, 155, 176, 176, 194, 194, 203, 203, 208, 209, 228, 229; (37), 116, 116, 118, 119, 160, 164, 172, 173, 212, 213; (38), 80, 80, 158, 158, 159, 160, 163, 163, 166-7, 167, 168, 168, 172, 172, 173, 177, 177, 194, 194, 208, 208, 216; (39), 160, 161, 161, 162, 162, 163, 163, 171, 171, 172, 173, 180, 180, 191, 191; (40), 216, 216; (41), 72-3, 73; (42), 216, 216, 217, 227, 227; (43), 160, 167, 215, 216; (44), 80, 81, 115, 115, 192, 192, 193, 193, 216, 216, 222, 222; (45), 80, 81, 192, 192, 218, 219, 225, 225; (46), 184-5, 185, 215, 238, 238; (48), 99, 105, 178, 179, 188, 188, 194, 194, 231-2, 236, 237, 238, 238; (49), 49, 238, 239; (50), 49, 68, 99, 132, 172, 232, 239, 239, 240, 240, 241; (54), 227, 227; (58), 227, 227
stars, shape of: crosses, 65, 65; 5 points (molet), 20, 21, 31-2, 37, 59, 64, 100; 6 points, 31, 32, 34, 34, 36, 41, 44, 44, 52,

52, 89, 89, 90-1, 91, 100, 121, 121, 189, 189; 7 points, 35, 35; 8 points, 14, 39, 39, 59, 59, 64, 88, 88; many points, 22, 23, 32, 41
"Stars and Bars," 130, 134, 135, 135, 136, 137, 138, 138, 140, 140, 141
"Stars and Stripes Forever" (Sousa), 186, 223
Star-Spangled Banner (flag), 29, 49, 52, 53, 99, 160, 223, 232
"Star-Spangled Banner" (poem and anthem; Key), 29, 49, 99, 232
Stiles, Dr. Ezra, 86
stripes: vertical, 19, 28, 28, 73, 75, 96; "war stripe," 59, 62, 62, 89, 89, 92, 93, 128, 128, 177, 177, 188, 188, 232; width regulated, 231; see also flag (and flag devices and motifs)
stripes, color of: blue and red, 22-3, 23, 39, 39, 44, 44, 190, 191; blue and white (or silver), 20, 21, 21, 22, 23, 24, 24; red and white, 43, 58; tricolor (red, white, and blue), 25, 59, 59, 60, 61, 61, 64, 84, 84, 190, 191; various colors, 22, 23, 24, 24, 25; white and red (heraldic order), 35, 35, 36, 36, 40, 40, 52, 52, 59, 59, 92, 92, 93
stripes, number of, reflecting current number of states in Union (or Confederacy), 25, 29, 41, 49, 51; (3), see "Stars and Bars"; (9), 19, 22, 23, 25, 27, 27, 63, 63, 93, 192, 192; (12), 25, 29, 40, 40, 41; (13), 43, 51, 54, 60; (15), 44, 44, 49, 51, 52, 52, 53, 71, 71, 99; (17), 26, 27, 89, 89
stripes, symbolism of, 19, 20, 25, 29
Stuart, Gilbert, 124
"Sullivan's Life Guard" standard, 22, 23
Svinin, Paul, Travels in North America, 92

T

Taft, William Howard, 105, 231
Tallmadge, Maj. Benjamin, 21, 39
Tammany Hall, 210, 211
"Tarleton's Terror," see Eutaw Flag
"Terry's Texas Rangers" banner, 138
textiles, tapestry, and needlework, 27, 78, 78, 94, 95, 130, 171, 171, 176, 176, 178, 178, 179, 188, 188, 190, 191, 191, 194, 194, 195, 195, 197, 197, 211, 211, 220, 220-1, 224, 224; British, 23, 23, 32, 40, 40; Chinese, 92, 93, 94, 95; French, 36, 36, 234, 235, 236, 237
"Third Flag," 54, 100, 123, 160
Third Maryland Regiment, see Cowpens Flag; star patterns, "Third Maryland"
"thirteen," symbolism of, 19, 63; see also stripes; stripes, number of, (13)
Thirteenth Regiment Flag, 16
Thompson, J. R., signature, 218, 219
Thomson, Charles, 47
Three Flags painting, 238, 238
Tillinghast, Joseph S., 191